Joy and Suffering

Joy and Suffering
My Life with ALS

Martin J. D'Amore, M.D.

2014

For Kirsten—wife, mother, acrobat.
And our children, Cecilia, William, and Martin (Jack)—
Bearers of Christ and endless potential

CONTENTS

FOREWORD

When I first saw Marty D'Amore, I was giving a presentation on bio-ethics at my parish, and Marty hobbled in on a cane. A few months later, he attended another presentation on bioethics. This time he entered the room in a motorized wheelchair. For me it was rather unnerving to be able-bodied, in good health, and speaking about ethical issues so closely related to the suffering of the sick, while Marty, someone clearly suffering from a debilitating disease, was there listening intensely. I couldn't help wondering what it was like to be grappling with these issues "from the inside"—so to speak.

Marty and I met soon afterwards. We discussed our common interests and goals: we were both striving to be good husbands and fathers. Marty recounted stories of work and play around the horse farm where he and his family live. He spoke about arranging horse jumps for his daughter Cecilia, clearing brush from the woods behind the house, laying up firewood for the winter, cleaning out the horses' stalls, and myriad other chores. In our discussions about bioethics he drew upon his medical expertise, built up over eleven years as a successful, interventional radiologist.

Marty was also interested in my literary and theological background. He asked me to read the rudiments of his spiritual autobiography. I asked questions that prompted him to think more deeply about the meaning of the joys and sufferings he was experiencing. At times I felt as though I was giving him "work" to replace the professional life lost to ALS. And what a "worker" he has been! The spiritual autobiography you are about to read was dictated through an iPhone into emails, initially, and then into a document that was edited by Christian Tappe of St. Benedict Press.

In many ways, Marty is a typical American guy, but there is definitely something special about him. He is inspired by the meaningful lives other people lead, for example, by the doctors who first showed him the beauty of a medical career and motivated him to pursue it. He has been given given plenty of natural intelligence and talent, and as a young man he struggled to discover and develop himself. He worked hard at his profession, marveled at the good he could do with it, and reaped its rewards. He has been wildly successful—by American standards—in his profession, family, and lifestyle.

More importantly, Marty demonstrates a kind of spiritual excellence. Not the spiritual excellence of the great ascetics of history, who master temptation with an iron will honed through self-denial. Rather the spiritual excellence of one who has prayed with a child's trust for a good life, lost himself in the confusion of growing up, found the way his talents could lead to success, and finally, as he achieved success, recognized something missing even before detecting the first symptoms of ALS. ALS focused his heart and mind on another kind of success: developing spiritual maturity. By slowly eliminating his physical mobility, ALS forced Marty to find new ways to love his wife, children, and friends. This book offers Marty's explanation of what he has learned in the hope that his family can discover, with him, some joy within the tragedy that has befallen them all.

Spiritual conversion is the stuff of great literature and epic poetry, but we are not usually given the privilege of a guided tour of this process unfolding in the lives of our neighbors and friends. We all change profoundly as we move through life, and know that our neighbors change in similar ways, but rarely do we get the opportunity to understand that change from the inside. In *Joy and Suffering: My Life With ALS*, Marty describes the experience of suffering with ALS, depicting not only the intricacies of the disease but also the hard-won meaning of the suffering it has brought him and his family.

Grattan Brown
Belmont Abbey College
Feast of the Immaculate Conception
December 8, 2013

PREFACE

Remember that you have only one soul; that you have only one death to die; that you have only one life, which is short and has to be lived by you alone; and there is only one Glory, which is eternal. If you do this, there will be many things about which you care nothing.
—St. Teresa of Avila

I am writing this spiritual autobiography so that my loved ones can one day see the good in my illness—the good in all our suffering—and be better for it. It is natural, at first, to have feelings of anger or self-pity when we experience tragedy. I want my loved ones to grow from this experience in both character and spiritually. I believe that character and spirituality go hand-in-hand, you cannot have one without the other.

To a child and a spouse, having a father and husband with Amyotrophic lateral sclerosis (ALS) seems unfair. But, I want them to be able to see life as God does. I want them to look back and see how our journey through ALS has enriched our lives. I hope the process of watching their husband's and dad's body deteriorate will help my family further develop empathy, compassion, and charity. I hope that it helps further foster in them self-esteem and peace.

I am a once vivacious and capable father, husband, and physician, now trapped within a motionless yet listful body. Each new day, it seems, brings new limitations. My family is continually reminded of my progressive illness and is concerned about losing me.

They are the caregivers for a limp, 140-pound, total-needs infant with the awareness of a fully functional forty-seven-year-old mind. They also have to deal with the stress and complications of caring for someone who is ventilator dependent. My respiratory muscles have deteriorated to the point that I cannot take a breath without the aid of a ventilator. If I am left unattended and the tubing comes loose, or the mouthpiece moves out of reach or the batteries deplete, I will quickly suffocate. A minor auto accident would be fatal for me, but I do not let that stop me. I try to remain a part of their lives as much as I can. This usually means several trips a day in our van. In the two-and-a-half years since we have owned our van, I have been loaded and unloaded seven thousand times according to the digital counter on my van lift.

As demanding as it is to care for an infant child, it is often more difficult to care for an ALS patient. I can only imagine the daily burden that falls primarily on my wife, Kirsten, my three children, Cecilia, William, and Jack, and my caregivers, McKenzie, Neil, Maggie, Megan, and Denise. Remove all the joy a parent gets in seeing their child reach new milestones and replace it with all the heart-wrenching stress of watching a husband and father reach his milestones in an accelerated inverse manner. They feed me, give me my medication, adjust my ventilator and my hands and feet, help me go to the bathroom, and do a thousand other things. They are learning to care for someone they love and for someone who cannot take care of himself.

I hope that the good they learn from taking care of me will blossom, giving them courage and fortitude during life's inevitable setbacks and tragedies.

I hope that they are learning from me how to handle and accept inevitable setbacks and tragedies, in the same way that I have come to accept my many blessings. I want them to have peace as they go forward in their lives. I am trying to give them an example of someone who is happy even as ALS has robbed me of my career, hobbies, and independence, and soon will rob my family and friends of me.

As my body has deteriorated, I have struggled to continue to play the role of parent, disciplining and setting limits. I have been tempted to start playing the role of grandparent, letting them do whatever they want so that they cultivate happy memories of me. But I have realized that the short term gain would cheat them in the long run.

Fatigued, I continue to participate in their extracurricular activities. It is hard to be social with the other parents, friends, when my whole body feels achy from a long, motionless day in my chair.

The world teaches us to value people by their abilities and productivity. Sometimes I feel less valued as I can no longer physically do anything other than give instruction or encouragement and say I love you. I want to show my family the value in someone who can do nothing for himself; who cannot be "productive" in a worldly sense.

Still, I hope that putting down my story and my struggles here will prove to be productive for my family, for myself, and for others who are enduring great suffering. While I have always gravitated towards mathematics and the sciences, English, literature, and grammar came less naturally to me. In telling my story, I am in unfamiliar waters. For the past year or so, I have been dictating notes in my phone to be read by my family someday. They are, I hope, pearls of wisdom which they are not yet ready to understand. A close childhood friend, Tim Lyne, encouraged me to compile some of these thoughts, and so here they are in book form. I am grateful to Tim for his challenge and encouragement. I am also indebted to my friend Grattan Brown, S. T. D. Without his guidance my story could not have developed early on. Christian Tappe has turned out to be so much more than an editor. He has helped me articulate my thoughts, giving them a coherent form.

This process of developing my thoughts and reflecting on my life has been tremendously therapeutic. And I hope that it will prove helpful to my family, friends, and others who grapple with suffering.

CHAPTER ONE

A DREAMER AND A PRAYER

Our prayer doesn't move God, rather our prayer is God praying through us prompting us to ask for the right things, In line with His own will. This is why we should end each prayer with "Thy will be done". He knows what we need even when it is not what we want. He knows us better than we know ourselves, our tiny inexperienced minds. Which is why He is being a loving parent when He doesn't give us what we want. How do we know what is best for us in the grand scheme. What is best may correspond with our prayer or may not.
—St. Thomas Aquinas

I was born in the groundbreaking year that construction began on the World Trade Center and my first son was born nine days before the towers came down. I was the fifth of seven children, born into a Catholic family from humble beginnings. As a boy, I was known as the inquisitor. My desire for knowledge—for figuring out why things were the way they were and how they could be better—was limitless, or at least it seemed that way to family and friends on the receiving end of a steady stream of questions. I often found myself in a day-dream of discovery, imagining ways to improve my world. As I got older and my world expanded, my thoughts moved to higher things like solving world hunger and world peace, as well as peace within my family.

1

Sometimes this thirst for knowledge brought unsavory results. I remember finding an old screwdriver with a worn wooden handle. A baby Robin had fallen breaking its wing. My mom and siblings said there was nothing we could do for it. I was young, seven– or eight-years-old. Forever curious, I saw an opportunity to see what was inside. I wanted to know how it all worked, the chirping, moving, flying. When I saw the blood and beating heart, I was mortified. To this day, I am a bit unsettled over what I had done.

A few years later, I was fascinated with fire. I filled up my new black squirt gun with water, snuck a pack of matches and slipped under our front porch when no one was looking. Earlier, while playing hide and go seek, I noticed a nice supply of dry autumn leaves. I separated a few from the pile and carefully burned them. I added a few more leaves and then I squirted the fire out with my gun. I melted a good portion of the squirt gun in the process. No longer able to squirt the fire out I put the matches back and hid my melted gun behind a toy beside our bathtub. It was an amateur move. Not long later the fire trucks came. My sister, Georgia, smelled smoke, thank goodness. There was no damage to the house, but I developed a healthy respect for fire.

                ***   ***   ***

In 1976, when I was ten years-old, my parents came into a small inheritance and purchased a modest summer cottage in Grand Beach, Michigan, on the southeast shore of Lake Michigan. I cherished those summers in Grand Beach during my adolescent and teen years. Valued friendships, formed over those summers of discovery and coming-of-age, persist to this day.

It was there that I had my first taste of affluence. As an adolescent, I did not ponder why other families had bigger houses and nicer things than we did. I was not jealous. That would come later.

I dreamed of a better life, however. I dreamed of a life that brought peace to my family and gave me a future of independence while satisfying my innate desire for inquiry. But I also frequently prayed for others. I had a profound sense God's presence and shared a discourse with Him at various moments of each day. I vividly remember a cold January afternoon like it was yesterday. It was 1980; I was thirteen years-old and in eighth grade.

Some of my siblings and I were waiting for my mom to pick us up after school. I came in from the cold to wait in our empty school chapel. I found myself drawn from the atrium into the nave, and I knelt in a pew. I did not pray for stuff. I specifically remember praying that I was not concerned about the little things. I found myself praying for the future, a wife and children, a happy loving family, a meaningful and fulfilling career and life.

I attended Fenwick high school in Oak Park, Illinois. Fenwick is a Catholic high school blocks from the west side of Chicago run by Dominican priests, Black Friars. It is a wonderful school. I owe much of who I am today to those formative years. Discerning a vocation to the priesthood came to a head on a pilgrimage to Rome my senior year with some of my Latin classmates. It was a most powerful week, but I believe that God already had a plan for me. He was going to see to it that my eighth-grade prayer would come to fruition.

At first, the allure of the carefree excess that I was initially exposed to during those summers spent in Grand Beach, Michigan only tapped at the periphery of my consciousness. By college, however, the centrifugal force of material desires penetrated to my core. It wasn't all material, however. A culture of tolerance and acceptance dove-tailed into relativism. The Philosophy of relativism is dangerous to a young mind, shaking the foundation of one's faith.

Unfortunately, since that heartfelt prayer I made in eighth grade, my soul steadily grew distant from God and the spiritual life.

CHAPTER TWO

SEARCHING FOR INSPIRATION

You can't get enough of what you don't really need.
—U2

My parents had several close childhood friends. Many of them, the ones I knew best, were successful commodities traders at the Chicago Board of Trade. It afforded them a good quality of life. The trading floor closed at 1:15 p.m., and all of them seemed to make a comfortable living. So, naturally, when I enrolled at the University of Illinois, Champaign-Urbana, I studied commodities trading and economics. I became more interested in achieving an affluent lifestyle and less concerned with how I did it. In fact, my goal was to find a path to this lifestyle with the least effort possible.

My mother, knowing my love of the sciences going back to my junior high years when I competed in the state science fairs, encouraged me to think about pre-med courses. She wanted me to consider a career in medicine. The pre-med students in my fraternity, however, had very different study habits and course requirements then I did. They were dissecting pigs on Friday afternoons while I was at happy hour. Additionally, for whatever reason, I did not think I had the aptitude or discipline to become a physician. I was lazy and content, sheltered by the world of campus life. Also, not having a physician or healthcare worker as a role model, I lacked the inspiration.

My parents went through a turbulent two year divorce during my college years which played a part in defeating my spirit and outlook. Drinking and partying became the salve for my pain. I went from the Dean's list to an average student overnight. I would not return to the Dean's list until my senior year. It was a chance encounter with the band U2, of all things, that jump-started the rehabilitation of my self-esteem.

A few years earlier, my younger brother Tom, in high school at the time, turned me on to their music. I was immediately hooked, enamored by the rawness of their lyrics. When I was a senior, Tom entered the University of Illinois as a freshman. On October 22, 1987, U2 performed at our Assembly Hall. The show was powerful and Bono's charisma was moving. A group of friends and I headed over to the University Inn where it was thought that the band was staying.

When we arrived, the lobby was packed with fans buzzing about the show. After about an hour of waiting, the crowd left and went to another hotel across campus. I convinced a friend, Bob Faust, to stay back with me. It was a decision we would not regret. Not five minutes after the crowd left, the band appeared from the elevator and the hotel manager unlocked the bar. Bob and I bought a beer and sat nervously at a table watching the band members drink beer and play darts.

My brother Tom soon arrived, and I gave him some money and told him to buy two shots of Irish whiskey and do one with Bono. I was chicken. Before long, they went back to their rooms. A few minutes later, however, the band called down to the hotel manager to see if we were still there. They wanted to experience a toga party and they wanted us to deliver them to a sorority. They soon reappeared from the elevator wearing togas. The Edge was carrying a stack of pizzas.

Bono led the way as they walked towards the hotel exit. Frozen in the moment, we remained seated. Bono leaned back into our view and nodded his head for us to come along. My brother and I, flanking Bono, let him carry the conversation. Eventually, Tom initiated a conversation about "40," one of their signature songs. He recently learned that the song was inspired by Psalm 40. After talking about the lyrics, Bono told my brother he was "top of the class."

It was 1 or 2 a.m., nevertheless, there were still students walking the streets. My brother and I were beside ourselves when Bono covered his face with his white toga and began singing their iconic song, "With or Without You," to the unsuspecting students. His voice was unmistakable, but with his face covered up they simply laughed. This happened a few more times before we reached our destination, the Delta Delta Delta sorority. We knocked at the front door.

Annoyed, a young lady answered and told us that it was too late for us to come in. Bono had his face covered at the time. When she started to close the door, however, Bono pulled the sheet from his face. She began screaming and threw the door open. Bono and the Edge found a piano, and before long, the previously quiet and empty first level of the sorority was electrified, as young ladies poured from their rooms. The Edge played "Hey Jude" while Bono sang-along, modifying the lyrics in a roast of Edge. On this night, college girls in nightgowns were no match for my attention.

The chance meeting lasted until the early hours of the morning when we finally went our separate ways, me to my reality and they to theirs, or so I thought. The next morning I was still in disbelief over what had occurred just a few hours prior. Busting with energy, I went for a walk. I started for the campus Union to get some money for the week. Hoping lightning would strike twice, I gravitated instead toward the University Inn.

When I arrived, I found a large crowd of students lined up to meet the band members. Word of our night-long escapade had gotten out. A friend towards the front of the line called me over and peppered me with questions about what had happened. Just then, Bono, Edge, Adam, and Larry exited the hotel. They looked exhausted from the tour, not to mention their late night. Bono caught sight of me, grabbed me by the arm, and allowed me to escort them to their waiting limousines. I think they saw an opportunity in greeting me to avoid the crowd. It was yet another surreal moment. They signed my student ID, thanked me, complemented our campus, and left. There were some disappointed people in the crowd after they left, and there was some contempt directed at me.

This unlikely encounter with my musical heroes invigorated me. More importantly, it reaffirmed that I had control over my destiny. Now anything was possible, I just had to reach out and grab it. Before, I was confused and my career path was uncertain. Afterwards, my renewed spirit started me down the road, although circuitous, to medical school.

***   ***   ***

During my senior year in college I became interested in commercial real estate, and later that summer, following my graduation in 1988, I was to begin a career in commercial real estate sales. Meanwhile, my uncle set me up with a job re-stacking pallets of one-hundred-pound sacks of sugar damaged by forklift drivers at his warehouse. This demeaning, backbreaking work sparked ambition. I was reminded of my eighth grade prayer, and I prayed for the future.

Earlier that summer, I had met two young physicians, the parents of one of the children in my mom's home daycare. I had extensive conversations with them about their careers, and, coupled with my mom's encouragement, they spurred me, to pursue a career in medicine. I finally felt inspiration and purpose. It was none too soon, as I was anxious about starting a career in commercial real estate sales. It felt empty, and this gave me an out.

I chose to forgo a steady paycheck and independence, and instead stayed in my childhood bedroom and focused on fulfilling requirements to apply to medical school. It was surprisingly effortless, despite knowing that my childhood and college friends were having a legendary time living in Chicago. Equally as surprising, the prospect of years and years of study, countless exams and possible failure in my quest stirred-up little anxiety within me. I was focused and finally found, by the grace of God, the confidence that eluded me for so long.

Through the turmoil, temptation, confusion and doubt, steadfast prayer gave me clarity, patience and perseverance.

CHAPTER THREE

RELAPSE AND GROWTH

Peace demands the most heroic labor and the most difficult sacrifice. It demands greater heroism than war. It demands greater fidelity to the truth and a much more perfect purity of conscience.

—Thomas Merton

My mom died on April 26, 1992. Her battle with breast cancer began as I entered medical school in 1990, and she died at the close of my second year. Her death was a real blow. Although I was closer to my mom than I was to anyone else, she slipped away before I could adequately express how grateful I was to her for her sacrifice, wisdom, and love. I had been in denial about the severity of her condition.

Feeling like I let her down, I cried for two days. I felt alone, deserted for the first time in my life. Final exams for second-year medical students had just finished up and it was six weeks before my first medical board exam. My classmates were studying ten to twelve hours a day. Numb with grief, all I could do was stare out the window and walk aimlessly. For six weeks I did not open a book. Somehow I passed the exam, but the loneliness and grief remained.

My mother was frail and weak over her last several months. She had distant metastases to her liver and bones. As a medical student, I knew what that meant. It meant a matter of *when*, not *if*. Unfortunately, I did not spend much time considering her inevitable death,

11

the pain was too great. Perhaps I was hoping subconsciously for a miracle. When I received the call that she had passed away early on the first Sunday morning after Easter, I was crushed. Alone and confused, I was lost all over again.

My mom taught me many life lessons including the value of friendships and education. A close childhood friend, Sean Briody, reminded me how my mom nurtured friendships for my siblings and me. She knew and understood the importance of strong life-long relationships, an understanding only someone who had those friendships could truly appreciate. Those friends helped her cope with her divorce and her bout with breast cancer.

At mom's funeral, Maureen O'Bryan, one of her childhood friends, gave an unforgettable eulogy. After reminiscing about some childhood memories, she closed her remarks by saying, "Dolores taught us how to die." This statement resonated with me as I dealt with the loss of her friendship and guidance at such a crucial time in my coming to adulthood.

A few weeks before she died we took a family trip to St. Pete Beach, Florida. Our family spent most Easters there, dating back to my early childhood when my dad's mother moved there. By this time mom was weak and frail, but she hid her suffering from us. I did not find out until later that she was experiencing significant pain from the bone and liver metastases.

Mid week during our stay, mom had me drive her to a hospital in Bradenton Florida where her doctor arranged for her to receive a platelet transfusion. I remember complaining to my mom that I was experiencing anxiety triggered by driving over the Sunshine Skyway Bridge. In retrospect, this anxiety was the expression of the early stages of my overactive thyroid gland, and yet it was nothing compared to the pain my mom was experiencing. Despite the morbid circumstances, I look back upon that day with fond memories. Feeling lousy and facing her mortality, she made it a wonderful day. It was capped off by a prime rib dinner on Longboat Key, just the two of us.

One morning, mom and I went for a walk on the beach. She

was weak, and a central venous catheter hung from her chest, however, she was determined to spend quality time alone with each of us. We talked about the future. She was proud of the fact that I was in medical school and was excited for me. Years back, she told me that she had dreams of studying medicine. She said that I would possibly marry a doctor. She was prophetic or maybe I was influenced by her suggestion, maybe both. "You will have a wonderful life, although there will be struggles and disappointment. There always are," she said. She was saying goodbye.

I recall one evening on that trip, my mom was sick to her stomach in the parking lot while we were waiting to be seated at a favorite restaurant in Pass-a-Grille. She sat through the meal with a smile and never complained. She wanted us to enjoy our final vacation with her and have one more happy memory of her. That experience came back years later to help me cope with my own illness and prognosis.

CHAPTER FOUR

PRAYER ANSWERED, MINE AND HERS

Our body has this defect that, the more it is provided care and comforts, the more needs and desires it finds.

—St. Teresa of Avila

Twelve years after my mother died, I was in my late thirties and just hitting my stride. My wife, Kirsten, and I had just had our third child and moved into our dream home, a small horse farm at the edge of town. We were settled into our careers. I had become an interventional radiologist, and my wife, who I met in medical school had become a physiatrist, an MD specializing in rehabilitative medicine. It takes a few years to make the transition from training in academia to the pace of private practice. I was reunited with some old hobbies and introduced to new ones. Our children were beginning to take up hobbies of their own: tennis, swimming, soccer, baseball, basketball, snow skiing, and horseback riding. We were tickled. We were in love and felt unfairly blessed.

I remember several conversations with Kirsten where we would just sit and talk about our many blessings, a strong marriage, healthy

happy children, rewarding careers, good friends, and fulfilling hobbies. I had achieved the very happiness I had prayed for as a child. My
family and I were finally getting to enjoy the fruits of life that were
nurtured through years and years of study, training (eighty– to one-
hundred-hour work weeks), and countless exams.

The great sacrifice and delayed gratification made the fruits that
much more satisfying. Still, I asked why we were so fortunate while
friends and acquaintances suffered financial problems, infidelities, divorce, illness, and untimely death. Why were we blessed to be so happy and content while people all over the world suffered from severe
poverty, the devastation of natural disasters, and atrocious violence?

We were happy, yet I was restless, hungry for something more. I
was gifted with an intimate understanding of human anatomy, physi-
ology, and pathology. I developed the skill set to diagnose and treat
disease as well as alleviate pain through image guided procedures and
I was provided with a wonderful arena in which to implement my
knowledge and skills. Nevertheless, I felt an emptiness and a yearning
to do something more, to somehow give back to the less fortunate.
Perhaps, I just felt guilty because the intellectual rewards were so great
and the quality of life so pleasing.

At the same time, I was upset with myself for being envious of
others. I was jealous of others' golf games or financial situations,
even though I was more well-off and had more free time than most
of my friends and acquaintances. I struggled with this internal battle
between charity and materialism. The allure of excess and indulgence
was winning out.

***   ***   ***

Even if we are lucky enough to achieve our dreams or even exceed
them, we want more: more stuff; more recognition; more abilities;
more free time; more gratification. It is a never-ending cycle that
won't stop until it consumes our souls. We obtain a material goal or
desire only to find that the satisfaction is ephemeral. Our attention
and desires move on to the next thing. A modest summer cottage was

once all we needed. Once acquired, our desires turn to a nicer home in a nicer location, waterfront perhaps. The same is true for clothes, cars, boats, vacations, and even, sadly, spouses.

Yes, I was caring for the sick, but I was being rewarded with professional creativity, intellectual challenges, and a quality of life that surpassed my dreams. And still, I found myself intrigued and jealous of colleagues who were taking annual trips to treat those in third world countries. Unfortunately, my profession as a radiologist is not in demand in third world countries where they cannot afford preventative medicines let alone medical imaging. I prayed for clarity and strength to follow through with my calling.

As a radiologist, my job was to look inside the human body in order to diagnose disease or injury, stage cancer, and survey for recurrent disease through a variety of imaging technologies: X-ray, fluoroscopy, angiography, MRI, ultrasound, CT scan, and nuclear medicine. Through image guided procedures, I obtained tissue for pathology and aspirated various fluids for histology and microbiology. Radiologists are trained to detect the spectrum of disease in all of its forms and stages throughout the body. Referring physicians rely on our recommendations for treatment and followup, as much as our interpretations. The work of a diagnostic radiologist is intense as our interpretation heavily impacts patient care. Our interpretations influence which patients get admitted, discharged, go to surgery and referred to a specialist.

As an interventional radiologist, I had the additional responsibility and privilege of treating patients with a vast array of disease processes, some iatrogenic. Many of the procedures involved opening arteries and veins closed by a myriad of etiologies. Likewise, I would close arteries and veins for an extensive list of pathologies. I created new blood flow passageways within the liver and gained direct access to the kidneys, liver, gallbladder, stomach, thorax, abdomen, and pelvis.

Armed with countless needles, catheters, guide wires, angioplasty balloons, stents, coils, particles, dyes, medications, state-of-the-art equipment, first class technologists and nurses not to mention, years and years of experience, I developed an unshakable confidence that seems surreal to me now. I performed dozens and dozens of different procedures, each one tailored in advance by the patient's history and physical condition, but also by careful interrogation of the patient's prior radiologic imaging.

The more sophisticated procedures invariably reveal unique and not infrequently aberrant anatomy as well as challenging manifestations of pathology. Like a quarterback breaking down disguised defenses, successful procedures more often than not require intra-procedural audibles. Multiple audibles, in fact, are commonly necessary in any given procedure.

My training as an interventional radiologist fulfilled my creative side, giving me the skills to treat disease and relieve pain with image-guided procedures. The procedures were intellectually demanding, and drew on my problem-solving skills, and hand-eye coordination. The job was intense because errors in judgement or technique could be catastrophic for the patient. Consultation with patients, primary care physicians, and specialists throughout the day made the job intellectually stimulating and personally rewarding. The wonder and power of healing sustained me in those long days and nights at work in the hospital.

My job as a physician allowed me to care for the sick and suffering. Although much of the work was charitable since many patients were uninsured and could not pay out of pocket, I was still well compensated. I felt guilty that I was not doing more with my wealth and time off. Perhaps if I were a primary care physician and developed long-term relationships with my patients, I would not have felt that way. I am afraid, however, that even that would not have filled the void.

The pace of my medical practice as with most medical practices, did not allow time to empathize with patients. The unfortunate insidious dehumanization of patients is necessary for survival. Dehumanization is a shield that allows us to keep up with the heavy daily workload and also allows us to perform procedures clearly, without emotional attachments. Sometimes dehumanizing a patient or patient's family can be difficult. Sadly this dehumanizing mindset too often spills over and affects interactions and relationships within and outside the workplace. Meanwhile, this nagging desire to help the less fortunate remained. I knew there was a deeper meaning to life. I had a deep sense of an unmet purpose and unmet potential. I was seeking God's will for my life.

Sometimes I felt the joy of caring for others. Sometimes I felt guilty that the personal rewards were so great. Mostly, I was caught up in the worldly things, distracted with hobbies, vacations, and investments. My work schedule was such that I would often work for two and a half weeks straight, including weekends, followed by one and a half weeks of rewarding myself for my hard work. My life was stuck in a rut, cycling between hard work and hedonism. At least my free time and indulgences centered on my family. It was this time that I valued most.

I had a premonition that some tragedy was sure to befall our family and disrupt our unfair good fortune. I can remember praying that it would be me. Be careful what you pray for. . . .

Chapter Five

Perception, Perplexities, Peace:
A Scramble for Lasting Memories

Yesterday is gone. Tomorrow has not yet come. We have only today.
Let us begin.

—Mother Teresa

In January 2007, Kirsten noticed fasciculations (muscle twitches) on my chest and arms. She was terrified and wanted me to see a neurologist. I was dismissive, attributing it to a thyroid condition that had been diagnosed and treated years before.

I cannot recall the precise date I first noticed the muscle cramps. Their onset was insidious. Although I had been experiencing muscle cramps for some time, there is a date that is etched into my memory. May 10, 2008 was our second annual—and as it turned out, final—camp out on the farm. We had roughly thirty-five families for dinner. Our friends, Valerie and Quintin Shuler, started smoking the Boston butts at 6 a.m. We threw a few dozen chicken breasts on later in the afternoon. Before dinner we had a memorable softball game. After dinner we had a large bonfire. Twenty-two families—in twenty-two tents—stayed and camped out over night. It was quite a scene.

I was awakened in the early hours of the morning by a painful hamstring cramp. When I tried to stand up I developed a reciprocal cramp in the opposite hamstring. I laid there writhing in pain for some time. Desperate and not wanting to wake the family, I crawled from our tent back to the house on my hands and knees. By the time I got into my bed, the cramps eased and I fell fast asleep.

In November 2008 we were in San Diego for our twelfth wedding anniversary. Kirsten had a medical meeting, and I surprised her with diamond earrings. We attempted several runs together throughout Coronado Island and the city. The runs together became memorable walks as I quickly became short of breath. We told ourselves that the shortness of breath was related to a cold and the fact that I had not been sleeping well.

I wanted to tie the symptoms together into one neat diagnosis. I wanted it to be a thyroid condition. However, Kirsten's suspicion about a more terrifying disease weighed in the back of our minds.

Kirsten noticed that the fasciculations were getting worse. I noticed that the debilitating cramps were occurring more frequently. Kirsten insisted that I see a neurologist. Summer 2008, I reluctantly saw one. I was no hypochondriac. He reassured us that my muscle cramps and fasciculations were probably a benign process, although he thought we should consider an electromyography (EMG). I waited a year and a half get that EMG.

I was one of those doctors who make the worst patients. As I look back, maybe I was scared. I convinced my wife that the symptoms were related to my thyroid condition, and she decided that my thyroid dose was too high and convinced me to lower my thyroid replacement medication. Of note, my thyroid replacement dosage was unusually high, dictated by blood tests that I had had years prior. Eventually I became hypothyroid, which further zapped me of energy.

I finally saw an endocrinologist in January 2009, two years after noticing the fasciculations and muscle cramps. It had been ten years since I last saw an endocrinologist. She started me on a new thyroid replacement medicine, and this new-found energy helped me enjoy a "guys" trip to Big Sky Montana for a week of skiing and a Wilderness Medicine Course that February. We skied every day except one when nine of us snowmobiled through the Idaho wilderness, alongside Yellowstone National Park. It was an unforgettable week.

For our children's spring break that March we spent the week skiing in Utah, Canyons and Deer Valley. Our family ski vacations were vivid then and especially now in hindsight. Skiing was an exhilarating new hobby for me and our children. For Kirsten, it was a welcome return to her days on the ski club at the University of Pennsylvania. The grandeur and beauty of the mountains surpassed my imagination, and together with the stillness and quiet on those slopes, it was a surreal and spiritual time.

I felt a closeness to Heaven in those mountains, a feeling I would not experience again until I went on my pilgrimage to Lourdes. Enjoying those ski vacations with our young children and seeing their joy tickled us in a way that we had not experienced before. In 2009, our youngest, Jack, was five and we all skied together for the first time. The week was especially memorable for all of us.

One afternoon Kirsten and Cecilia hit the black diamond trails while I went with the boys. The plan was for William to lead the way, with Jack, who just turned five, in the middle, and with me trailing behind in case anyone fell. Well, Jack didn't get the memo. William headed down one trail while Jack continued along the ridge leading to an altogether different trail. My heart sank. I saw William stop and look back at me. I cannot imagine how he felt, deserted by his father. I will never forget the despair I felt when I left William, only seven years-old at the time, so I could catch up with Jack. By a small miracle, our trail led back into William's as he was passing by. William took it all in stride. Amazingly, he was not upset, confident that we would be at our emergency meeting place, the Tombstone chairlift.

It would be our fifth and final ski trip together as a family. In retrospect, I was not myself on those last two ski trips in 2009. My strength and endurance was not the same. Additionally, my poor night's sleep seemed worsened, exacerbated by the altitude, I expect.

I woke up multiple times a night. It would be another eleven months, November 2009, however, before I realized that I must have sleep apnea. Looking back, I should have put things together sooner. However, I was focused on work and family activities. I was not conditioned to focus on my own well-being.

***   ***   ***

We spent Easter break 2009 in Florida with family. It was there that I noticed a strange sharp pain in my mid chest while trying to jog on the beach with Kirsten. This pain felt different than a typical cramp. My endocrinologist assured me the symptoms were not related to the new thyroid medication as I had hoped. She recommended a cardiology consultation. As heart disease did not explain all of my symptoms, I was not convinced. The workup was negative. I was becoming a better patient.

Over the spring and the summer, I began to notice a sharp decline in my physical abilities. I lost significant distance on my golf shots. This dramatic change in my golf game, surprisingly, did not alarm me. Before a charity softball game also in spring 2009, I became winded with warm-ups and just playing catch. Additionally, I could barely hit the ball out of the infield. It was as if my core and respiratory muscles were significantly weakened while my other muscles remained strong. Stunned by it all, I could not put it together. I was not ready to throw in the towel, I remained hopeful that my weakness was thyroid related.

My ego told me that doctors are healers, we were doing God's work and should be immune from illness, although, I knew in my heart that we were just like everybody else.

***   ***   ***

In June 2009, we returned to Beaver Creek, Colorado, where our children attended the Suzuki Institute violin camp. Kirsten and I loved that our children played violin, while they merely tolerated it. But, we all looked forward to this camp. There is something majestic about violin in the mountains. The camp is very well organized with wonderful instructors and musicians from all over the country.

Not being a musician, I was always with my boys who were younger and less experienced. Kirsten stayed with Cecilia who was older and more advanced. Mornings were busy with large and small group classes. Each class is surprisingly memorable especially afternoons learning pennywhistle with Marybeth Norris. I will never forget escaping for lunch one day with my youngest, Jack. We took the chairlift up to the top of the mountain where we had a delicious lunch then played in a patch of residual snow. Late afternoons meant s'mores at a fire pit outside our hotel and evenings were spent ice skating. Violin was never so much fun.

I am not sure why, but one night I decided to weigh myself on the scale in our hotel room. I was shocked to see that I had dropped thirty pounds since my January visit to the endocrinologist. I looked at myself in the mirror and could see my entire rib cage front to back. I was concerned. I had been physically fit, so I knew that the weight-loss must have been largely muscle mass.

I experienced this unusual weight loss once before, at the end of my third year of medical school. I was in my surgical rotation and experiencing anxiety and restlessness. I was eating several entrées at each meal. Despite this increased appetite and caloric intake, classmates were noticing that I was looking thin. At first, I assumed the weight-loss was related to the demands and long hours of my surgical rotation. I was more concerned about the anxiety and restlessness.

I saw a school counselor who wanted to start me on an antidepressant. Maybe he was influenced by the loss of my mom the year prior. A little bit of knowledge can be dangerous, but something did not sit right with me. As fate would have it, the summer before, I had done thyroid research with an endocrinologist, Dr. Dwarakanathan. Although uncommon in young males, I thought that Graves' disease of the thyroid gland might be the culprit.

I went to see Dr. Dwarakanathan, and he confirmed my suspicions; I was diagnosed with Graves' disease, a condition where the thyroid gland over produces a hormone that regulates the body's metabolism. The diagnosis explained my anxiety and weight loss despite my increased appetite. Interestingly, I lost thirty pounds then as well.

In June 2009, my endocrinologist changed my thyroid medication once again when we returned from Beaver Creek. I remember the uncomfortable feeling at Mass of the wooden church pew against my spine, exposed by the muscle wasting. Kneeling triggered hamstring cramps. To combat this, I alternated kneeling on one knee at a time. One leg would be stretched out relieving the cramp while the other hamstring was in spasm. This dance continued until I transitioned to a wheelchair and would kneel no more.

I tried to rebuild muscle mass with aggressive eating and anaerobic exercise. In retrospect, I did not have the hyperphagia that I experienced with Graves' disease in medical school. Eating became a chore. Kirsten encouraged me to stop by the YMCA after work to rebuild my muscle mass. I had always welcomed opportunities to exercise, but the frequent muscle spasms—at rest, while stretching, and on exertion—along with the shortness of breath made it onerous. I also felt guilty missing out on family time.

***   ***   ***

We started taking more vacations—eleven in the fourteen months leading up to my eventual diagnosis. These vacations demonstrate my commitment to this world, the tangible. But also, they are like snapshots in the photo album of life. Life seems to slow down allowing for reflection. Routines and technologies are left behind and replaced by adventure, discovery, and imagination. Sharing this enhanced time together without distractions of friends and work never disappointed. I had a tremendous need to create lasting memories with my family. Our children were young and did not yet suspect any trouble.

In July, we found ourselves in Yellowstone and the Grand Teton National Parks. I was not feeling well but I was not going to let that stop me. I relished the opportunity for one more adventure vacation with my family. It would be my last.

We enjoyed many hikes together. Our tour guides planned a hike through a rolling meadow leading to a field of boiling mud springs before reaching a trail along the rim of the Grand Canyon of Yellowstone. It was bison mating season, and when we arrived at the beginning of the hiking trail, we saw a bison shredding the bark off a few trees thirty yards from us. He was leaving his scent. We waited for him to move along before we started on our adventure, with bison nearby throughout the hike.

Our guides were extremely informative and reassuring, though one did tell us he saw a bison stare down a grizzly bear. We never would have considered such a daring hike without them. Our five year old Jack fell asleep in my arms as we reached the rim of the Grand Canyon of Yellowstone. The views were absolutely breathtaking. Kirsten and I were grateful that Jack was sleeping in my arms as the trail was extremely dangerous for a spirited five year old. He awoke as we approached a safe lookout point overseeing the upper and lower falls.

On the edge of town in Jackson, Wyoming, is a small mountain, you might call it a large hill compared to the Teton Mountains. Our children took the chair lift up the mountain with Kirsten's parents, while Kirsten and I hiked up. We each carried small backpacks and water canisters.

It was the last day of a most memorable week and I was exhausted. About a third of the way up, I was bent over and sucking wind. Another third and Kirsten had both backpacks and the water. I had to take several breaks to catch my breath. We began seeing several hikers who had passed us going up, now making their descent.

As dusk fell, a panic set in. Kirsten went ahead to see how much farther I would need to hike in order to catch a chairlift down. It was only several hundred yards, yet it seemed insurmountable. With much encouragement, we eventually made it to the chairlift. I was shaken. The denial was over. It was that fated hike that convinced me that something was really wrong. I pivoted away from hopes of thyroid complications to something much more terrifying.

By November 2009, one and a half years after my initial neurology consultation, and nearly three years after my initial symptoms, I finally began a definitive work up. I made an appointment with a neurologist in August, but, the earliest open slot was not until November. Relief from the suffering would have to wait.

Finally, my neurologist at Duke University Medical Center performed a thorough history and physical. I had blood tests. A neurology fellow performed an extensive electromyography study (EMG) where needles were placed into several muscles in my arms, legs, back, and tongue. An electric current was passed from the needle into my muscles and motor neurons. Despite concerns of a specific horrifying disease, we were reassured. The roller coaster of a work-up would take six months before the diagnosis finally came.

I kept myself busy with work, family, and friends. I never focused on the "what ifs." I was matter of fact to family, friends, and colleagues who were concerned with my choking spells and my weight-loss. Life was a real struggle physically, but I tried not to let speculation and emotions further compromise my role as husband, father, and physician.

Soon after my November neurology examination, my sleeping troubles progressed. Eventually it got to the point where I would wake up every hour with headaches. Perplexed, I was underweight and there was no family history, it was not until then that I realized I must have sleep apnea. The next day at work, I discussed my symptoms and thoughts with a pulmonologist friend. He gave me an overnight pulse ox recorder, a device that records my blood oxygen levels. The results were alarming. I notified a neurologist friend who gave me immediate access to a breathing device commonly known as a CPAP, for "continuous positive airway pressure." A sleep study later confirmed that I had central and obstructive sleep apnea.

The alarms took months to get used to for myself and Kirsten. The facemask made me claustrophobic and I needed to wear it so tight to prevent a leak that I had an open wound on the bridge of my nose. The wound was a little awkward, but I was desperate. Eventually we were getting a full night's sleep. The wound on my nose would remain until May 2010 when my new neurologist, Dr. Brooks, switched me to a ventilator and a new type of facemask. A scar remains, a reminder of the turmoil.

I saw several neurologists at Duke University Medical Center and the Mayo Clinic. There were MRIs, CT scans, blood tests, and several EMGs. I also underwent a muscle biopsy and a spinal tap. Kirsten was always there at my side. There were many tender moments as we anxiously explored the medical campuses in between appointments and procedures. We imagined what life may have been like if we opted for careers in academic medicine. We reminisced, holding onto hope and staying optimistic—outwardly anyway.

My wife and I flew separately back from Mayo Clinic. Although inconvenient, we always agreed on flying separately when traveling without our children. After two long days of testing, I caught an early flight home from Rochester Minnesota, soon after Kirsten's flight and prior to my closing meeting with my neurologist. I was anxious to get back to my family and felt certain of the diagnosis. I sat next to a wonderfully compassionate PhD from Mayo Clinic on his way to Chicago to give a presentation. It was the first time I verbalized my diagnosis to anyone including myself.

On April 26, 2010, I got the call from Dr. Laughlin, my neurologist at Mayo Clinic. It was eighteen years to the day of my mom passing from breast cancer. I remember a very pleasant conversation with Dr. Laughlin. I could feel her compassion over the phone as she told me I had ALS, what Kirsten had feared from the first symptoms more than three years prior. The denial was over. Believe it or not, I laid there on the sofa and felt a sense of relief. The burden from all of the struggles I endured over the past three years was strangely lifted. My suffering was real, the diagnosis now certain.

I could let down my guard. My mom was calling me home. I prayed, "Thy will be done," and I prayed for peace, strength, and courage. My last hope for a treatable disease was now transformed into hope for eternity in Heaven. This new vision brought renewed purpose for me as husband, father, friend, and Christian.

CHAPTER SIX

LIFE ACCELERATED

I know God won't give me anything I can't handle. I just wish he didn't trust me so much.

—Mother Teresa

ALS, also known as Lou Gehrig's disease, is a progressive debilitating disease that destroys the motor nervous system, insidiously, though sometimes it can come on very quickly, leading to paralysis and death. Every ninety minutes someone is diagnosed with ALS and every ninety minutes someone succumbs to the disease. The incidence is exactly equal to the death rate. This fact explains why this disease has such a low prevalence. There are only 30,000 people living in this country with ALS. Death comes three to five years from diagnosis, on average, usually a result of respiratory complications. I have been on a ventilator when sleeping since November 2009 and twenty-four-hour non-invasive ventilation since July 2011. Without the invention of CPAP devices and ventilators, I would have died prior to my diagnosis.

ALS is a pathologic marathon, the ultimate marathon, for the patient and the patient's family. I am cramping up, losing control of my body and I cannot catch my breath . . . all the while trying to enjoy each metaphorical step with my family and friends proud of me in the end.

Following the diagnosis, I told my wife this new journey together would be more difficult for her than for me. She would have to face the deterioration and inevitable demise of her husband, all the while fulfilling her duties to our three children as a mother and to her career as a physician. Additionally, she would have to take up duties formally mine as father and caretaker of the home and farm. And she would have to undertake all this while bearing much of the responsibility as my caregiver. This incredible burden would be compounded by the stress that my progressive illness would bring upon our family.

She has balanced all of this admirably. I am so grateful to her and count her and our three children as my greatest blessings. I love each of them with all my heart and would not want to make this journey with anybody else.

After my diagnosis, I tried to go about my business as I normally would. I experienced labored breathing with light exertion and choking fits and cramps in my abdominal muscles, legs, hands, and feet. They were distracting and painful. Nevertheless, they did not interfere with my job as an interventional radiologist. The lead apron that protected me from the fluoroscopy radiation during procedures became increasingly difficult to put on and wore heavy on my back. By the end, I was in agony. When I referred one of my favorite procedures, a transjugular intrahepatic porto-systemic shunt, to another hospital, I knew the end was near.

Tying my surgical mask triggered a spasm in my hands and eventually became impossible. Technologists and nurses were quick to help. However, spasms in my hands during procedures progressed. I would straighten out my bent fingers, waiting for the spasm to go away before I could continue with the procedures. I often joked about the hand deformities with my team, hoping to make light of the situation.

There was a tense moment for them, I am sure, when I could not release my grip on a scalpel. I never panicked. I knew the spasms would go away and I would be able to release the scalpel. I was very confident in my abilities; I simply took my time. The procedures always went smoothly, up to the very end when I gave up my interventional privileges. My technologists and nurses were incredibly patient and understanding while assisting me in those procedures.

I had the incredible clarity that comes with knowing that each procedure might be my last. I savored them. The memories are a joy, recognizing that my abilities were a gift. I became so grateful for the privilege of working with my radiology partners and with all of the physicians and staff at Gaston Memorial Hospital. We had an ideal work environment where we mentored each other. I have much gratitude to all of my radiology partners especially Mark Memolo, who had the biggest impact on my private practice career. Add this paragraph to follow: I am deeply grateful to all the countless physicians who have helped train me. There are too many mentors, professors, and physicians from Rush University Medical Center where I earned my medical degree and what an education it provided me. Drs. Marc Borge, Terry Demos, Bob Wagner and many others at Loyola University Medical Center who helped me build an incredible radiology foundation. Drs. Ruoth and Reagan and so many others at Wake Forest University Medical Center where I received extraordinary training as an interventional radiology fellow.

I had come a long way, from unlikely beginnings, to the fulfilling life I prayed for in the eighth grade. In fact, everything I prayed for that cold January afternoon came to fruition as the disease that would take it away revealed itself little by little.

As children we reach milestones, often unnoticed and rarely remembered or appreciated. As parents we rejoice when our children reach these. As we age, we gradually reach those milestones again in an inverse manner. With ALS, those reverse milestones are simply accelerated. We lose our ability to work, drive, dress, maintain our hygiene, go to the bathroom without assistance, walk, talk, eat, move, and breathe.

The problem is that those of us with ALS are not ready to lose so much so quickly. We do not have the cognitive impairment from brain atrophy or deterioration that comes with the normal aging process or other neurodegenerative diseases, relative to the rapid deterioration of our muscles. At first I was distressed at the prospect of maintaining my supratentorial function while my body failed. Now, I realize that it is a blessing and I would not want it any other way.

Without our muscles, we cannot take care of our needs and the needs of others. We become a thinking, loving, caring inanimate object with a singular desire. We want to hold and comfort our loved ones. We want to ease their pain, frustration, confusion, and anguish. We want to guide, mold, prepare, and share. We want to be one with them again in Heaven.

Take away the exhilaration a child or a parent experiences in reaching a milestone and add to that the anguish and frustration of trying to hold on to that ability once taken for granted. The more you try the more magnified the anguish and frustration becomes. The remaining weakened motor neurons have a progressively longer latency period before they can fire, triggering an anemic muscle contraction. Our loved ones have to watch us go through these unrelenting transitions. I cannot imagine how difficult it is for them.

The transitions were difficult for Kirsten each step of the way. I felt like I could let go and encouraged measures in anticipation of the transitions. Frustrations often centered around her resistance to my changing—and worsening—condition. Our spouses and children are not prepared emotionally to watch our steady deterioration and subsequent confusion, frustration, and anguish. How could they be? And through all this turmoil, they are asked to do the heavy lifting we once did and undertake the incredible task of caring for our ever increasing needs. It is easier to deal with my own suffering than to watch my family suffer.

I gave up my interventional radiology privileges at the hospital a few months after my diagnosis and a year after that I gave up my radiology career entirely. Each decision was painful, but I knew it was time. Really, it was no decision at all. ALS was in control. Interventional radiology had been my professional identity for eleven years. I loved it on so many levels. All at once, it was over.

Chapter Seven

Segue

True progress quietly and persistently moves along without notice
—Saint Francis of Assisi

In July 2010, my family and I went to Chicago to visit family and friends. A close friend, Fred Levy, organized a surprise two-day visit with ten friends from back home. I was touched by their sacrifice of time and money. It was a moving and memorable visit with great food and many laughs. The highlight was a trip to Wrigley Field to take in a Cubs game. The guys all pitched in for a donation to the Cubs charitable arm, which gave us access to the field and the Cubs' dugout.

Not long after my diagnosis, I developed foot drop and needed an orthotic brace to assist my ambulation. The orthotic made walking easier only to uncover worsening shortness of breath on exertion. I was getting winded walking from my car to the department of radiology and around the hospital. Joining our children at practices and games and getting around the farm was quickly becoming impossible.

Knowing how much trouble I was having with walking, Fred scheduled a Segway tour of the city and the lake front for the eleven of us. It was a three hour tour, which made me nervous as walking and standing were a struggle. I immediately felt comfortable on the

Segway. Able to stand up straight and keep my balance for the first time in months, I was hooked. Invigorated by this new-found freedom, I bought one as soon as I got back home. I had heard that my friends were going to pitch in to buy me one. Embarrassed by their generosity, I wanted to beat them to the punch. It gave me legs again, and my shrinking world was reopened.

The Segway allowed me to join my boys on our baseball field in a back pasture and my wife and daughter on the riding arena. I could ride the Segway out to our barn where Kirsten would assist me on and off our lawn mower. We had some scary moments, but I was not ready to let go of that duty. Kirsten knew how much I loved taking care of the farm and she wanted to help me maintain that ability and satisfaction as long as I could. By the end of the mowing season 2010, however, I felt unsafe on the mower, and another chapter was closed.

While ALS was taking various tasks and abilities away from me, the Segway helped me maintain my independence and allowed me to join my family on the pitch and at horse shows. I followed alongside on bike rides, mountain hikes, and walks on the beach. We all loved our family outings together. They were adventures that we could all have together. Distracted with nature, the kids always got along beautifully.

The Segway went wherever I did, including to work. It was a long distance from the parking lot to the radiology department. With the Segway, I made it work. I even used it to get around the hospital. I will never forget the looks I got when, wearing my white lab coat, I rode into the intensive care unit, performed a procedure, and left on the Segway.

The Segway helped make it possible for me to continue working for another year after my diagnosis. I needed that last year of work. There was too much change too quickly. That final year of work helped me come to terms with my new reality. It brought closure to another chapter of my life. What a blessed and glorious chapter it was.

The Segway even helped my family, friends, and I raise money for ALS. In October 2010 Kirsten and two good friends, Karen and Bill Hunter, trained for and ran the Chicago Marathon raising $43,000 for ALS research. It was Kirsten's third marathon, although she had not run one in sixteen years, when she was in medical school. As for Bill and Karen, it was their first marathon. It was another emotional time with tears shed by the four of us after the race.

The week before our trip to Chicago, I rode my Segway into the airport confirming that I would be able to take it with us on our trip. I could not walk more than a few hundred feet by this time. However, when I arrived with my family at our gate, me on my Segway, the airline officials told us the lithium-ion batteries could not be allowed on the plane. I was stunned as the Segway, my legs, were taken by security so that we could board the plane.

As soon as we landed in Chicago, I called the fellow who owned the Segway tour outfit in downtown Chicago. We became friendly during our tour a few months earlier, and he graciously let me rent one of his Segways for the weekend, something he had never done before. The marathon was on Sunday, and on Saturday morning we drove to South Bend Indiana to attend a Notre Dame football game.

It was a beautiful afternoon. We spent a few hours at the College Football Hall of Fame before heading over to the campus to tailgate with family and friends. My sister Michelle and her husband Pat prepared an amazing spread of food and beverages.

We then toured the campus, me on my Segway, highlighted by prayers in the Basilica of the Sacred Heart and at the grotto. I remember the goosebumps I got when Ceci expressed to me how she was struck by the beauty of the Basilica and hoped to one day attend Notre Dame as a student. My father and several friends were Notre Dame alumni, and so I had attended many games. Being on campus again brought back many old memories. My good friend Tim Quinn, an alum, pushed my wheelchair just in case I became fatigued on the Segway. My boys took turns as Tim entertained them racing through campus in the wheelchair. Initially, security would not let us into the stadium on the Segway. Tim explained the situation to security and eventually they acquiesced. I was told I was the first person to attend a game at Knute Rockne Stadium on a Segway! It was an exciting game with the Irish besting the University of Pittsburgh. The day is a precious memory for my family.

It was late when we finally got back to our hotel in Chicago. I don't know how Kirsten survived. It was a long and exhausting day with most of the burden falling on her. Kirsten had to get up the next morning and run the Chicago Marathon.

The plan was to meet up with Kirsten at mile thirteen in the heart of the business district to cheer her on. The kids and I were excited. We met up with my friend from high school, Jay Ward, and his wife Christine, a friend from medical school, along with their daughter Sophia. The crowd at this particular corner was massive. Even so, with the help of our children and my Segway, we were able to sneak through the crowd.

Before long we saw Kirsten and yelled to get her attention. Somehow, she heard us and ran over. She had the biggest smile on her face. Seeing us had energized her, and she looked great. I could not believe that she just run thirteen miles. We all got to give her a hug and take photos. We missed Bill and Karen Hunter in the crowd of runners. Our children and the Wards, me on my Segway, raced across town to mile marker twenty-five where another friend, Bill Caulfield, was holding tables for us and other friends and family at a street-side restaurant.

It was an unseasonably hot day with temperatures above eighty degrees. The runners looked exhausted, and several of them fell on the pavement right in front of us. At nearly four hours since the start of the race, I began to get anxious. We should have seen her by now. She had not trained for the race as much as we would have liked given all of her responsibilities.

But we soon spotted her, four hours after the start of the race. She was limping and exhausted. Her knee had started bothering her at the eighteen-mile mark. She ran over to us, we all hugged again and took pictures. She finished the race at four hours and twenty-five minutes. This was not her fastest time, but it was her most satisfying.

While everyone went to Mike Ditka's restaurant where we had planned a private party, I made my way through the crowd to return my Segway in Grant Park. There was a festival going on in addition to the marathon and the traffic was terrible. Unable to stand up straight, I was bent over on Columbus Drive trying to flag down a taxi. It took thirty agonizing minutes to flag down a vacant cab.

I thought I was going to collapse. But, it was hard for me to feel sorry for myself. Kirsten, after running the marathon went back to our hotel room, packed up all of our stuff, loaded it into our rental van and met us at the restaurant. She has an incredible drive and sense of duty.

When we finally arrived at Ditka's, Bill hugged me and wept. I will never forget it. He was physically and emotionally exhausted, yet he was exuberant at completing his first marathon and raising so much money for ALS research. I did not run a marathon. I didn't even take more than a few steps that day, and yet I felt terrible. Struggling to breathe and cramping, it was difficult for me to socialize. I did the best I could. Maybe a combination of the agony and joy allowed me to take in the celebration from outside myself. It was a surreal day, I remember every detail. It was an unimaginably wonderful weekend that will never be forgotten by any of us. Yet, it took great perseverance, mainly on Kirsten's part.

    ***   ***   ***

All things come to an end, however. By February 2011, I was no longer able to step up onto my Segway. I had been feeling unsteady on it for a while and it had become unsafe. It was a sad day when, seven months after it extended my independence and mobility, I sold the Segway. My world was drastically diminished literally overnight. I was grateful that the Segway gave me seven more months of independence. The Segway eased the segue to a power wheelchair as I was used to ambulating by way of a machine. At the time, I believed my independence was lost. Actually, lost independence was just beginning.

Not long after I moved to a wheelchair, I lost the ability to safely drive a car. Surprisingly, this lifestyle change stirred up little anxiety within me. Quitting, formerly alien to my modus operandi was getting easy. I felt like I was letting my family down, however, as I could no longer share in the load of shuttling our children to and from school and extracurricular activities. My last few months of work, Kirsten drove and assisted me onto my wheelchair. I was too fatigued and short of breath to be embarrassed.

Bathroom breaks were interesting. I parked my power chair outside the bathroom door in our angiography suite. With one hand on my cane and the other on the bathroom door, I would pull myself up and hobble into the bathroom. The angiography technologists and nurses were concerned I might fall. I left the door partially open in case I did. I used my cane to lift the toilet seat and again to lower it and flush the toilet when I was finished. I could not bend over. I had to hunch over onto the sink to wash my hands before hobbling, exhausted, back to my power chair.

Despite the physical difficulties, my mind was intact. Intellectually, I was able to perform my job as far as interpreting studies and consulting with other physicians. However, as my dexterity deteriorated, it became increasingly difficult for me to use the computers needed to interpret and dictate the studies. My productivity was progressively compromised. I finally went on disability in June 2011, a full year after I intended. My radiology partners, technologists, nurses, secretaries, and transcriptionists were both understanding and accommodating.

***   ***   ***

ALS took away my career and my independence, and now was going to teach the patience. I had always been in a hurry; always trying to accomplish things. I wanted quality time with my wife and children, I wanted to grow our radiology practice, and, of course, I wanted to improve my golf and tennis games. I became used to getting what I wanted although persistence and perseverance were sometimes necessary. It was now just me, my chair, my ventilator, and time. Empty time. Productivity, hobbies, and chores were no longer an option. To my mind, relaxation, reading, and writing were overrated was my mindset. It was yet another transition.

Life is a continuous series of segues. Under a microscope, we see a continuous series of denials, changes, successes, and failures strung together moment by moment. Turn down the power a little and we can see the seasons of life. Power down more still and we see generations, the rise and fall of nations, still more and we see the rise and fall of man. With the just the right perspective, we can begin to see how all these segues—these transitions, changes, setbacks, and success—come together in a life, moving us toward a singular end.

The best advice I can give ALS patients, my loved ones and anyone is to embrace transitions. Additionally, we must never lose sight of the fact that our lives have meaning no matter the condition or circumstances. Anticipation of and welcoming transitions all along the course of my physical deterioration has made the journey easier, even enjoyable. Segues have brought relief to my suffering. Disappointments, setbacks and tragedies are inevitable. We must push on and do what we ought to do for all suffering no matter the intensity or duration is nothing compared to the glory of God.

I am reminded of those famous words of the Serentiy Prayer: "Lord, grant me the serenity to accept the things I cannot change, the courage to change the things I can and the wisdom to know the difference."

Innocence, inquisitiveness, wonder, always wonder, acrimony, insecurity, searching, inspiration, grief, hard work, perseverance, love, family, fulfillment, hard work, success, confidence, Epicurean living, emptiness, seeking God's will, physical deterioration, mortal, spiritual rehabilitation, Lourdes, Order of Malta, ensuing infancy, fullness, jubilation, peace—segues in a life . . . a wonderful life.

CHAPTER EIGHT

LOURDES

Jesus said to the crowds, "Come to me, all you who labor and are carrying heavy burdens, and I will give you rest. Take my yoke upon you, and learn from me; for I am meek and humble in heart, and you will find rest for your souls. For my yoke is easy, and my burden is light."

—Matthew 18:28–30

I heard of the apparitions of Mary in Lourdes, France, from a good friend, Chuck Meakin. He is well-respected as a physician, not to mention a wonderful community leader, husband, father and friend. But, what strikes me most about Chuck is his incredible gift of compassion. This compassion of his was well-established long before he took up my cause. Soon after my diagnosis, he brought me Lourdes water, from a spring there, as well as several testimonials of their healing powers.

St. Bernadette uncovered the spring during one of eighteen apparitions she experienced. The fourteen-year-old peasant girl Bernadette Soubirous uncovered a spring, digging with her hands upon the direction of the Blessed Virgin Mary. She experienced all eighteen of her Apparitions in 1858 at a grotto on the banks of the Gave de Pau River. Initially, the grotto was boarded up by the city, but as the healing powers of the spring water spread, the grotto and spring were reopened to the public. Bathhouses fed by the spring were erected beside the grotto, and before long thousands from across Europe made the pilgrimage to Lourdes to drink and bath in the sacred spring waters. Today, six million pilgrims visit Lourdes every year.

I am one of those pilgrims. I am one of the sick who has travelled to that great shrine to Our Lady to seek healing, and I have found it. Although, I still have ALS.

During that first Advent after my diagnosis, the children and I arrived at Saturday evening Mass early so that we could go to confession. An acquaintance, Mary Thierfelder, seeing that I was having trouble standing up, gave me her seat in the front of line. Later, when I was praying, she reached out and gave me her Rosary. Mary told me that it was from Lourdes. I was touched by her sincere kindness and still treasure that Rosary.

One morning that December, I had the day off work and found myself at the 8 a.m. Mass. I regularly attended Mass on Sunday but rarely attended a weekday Mass unless it was a holy day of obligation. My good friend Chuck happened to have the day off and was at the same Mass. He stuck around after and we had a short chat. He wanted to get a Notre Dame blanket blessed by our priest, Father Arnsparger, as a gift to me.

While Chuck was waiting to get the blanket blessed, he began talking with the woman that gave me the Rosary a few weeks prior. He told her my story, and she asked if I would be interested in a pilgrimage to Lourdes with the Order of Malta. Chuck mentioned it to me, and I jumped at the opportunity. This pilgrimage was just what I needed.

Chuck and my good friend from medical school, Tim Quinn, were my companions on the week-long pilgrimage at the end of April and the first of May in 2011. Although Chuck was there for me emotionally, his job was to help out with the other *malades*. *Malades* are individuals with an illness making a pilgrimage to Lourdes in search of healing, both body and soul. I was a *malade*. A little secret I have learned, we are all *malades*, many of us just do not realize it.

Tim was my roommate and never left my side the entire week.

ALS was rapidly taking over my body by the time of the pilgrimage, and Tim helped me immensely. He assisted me with going to toilet, getting me on an off, and making sure I was clean after. He showered me and washed me. He brushed my teeth, help me get dressed in the morning and undress at bedtime. He was at my side for each meal, assisting me in lifting my fork and cup as I was too weak to do this on my own. He pushed me in my wheelchair all over Lourdes, amusingly, racing in and out of cramped elevators, the doors of which closed seemingly without pause. It was all incredibly humbling yet beautiful.

As my muscles weakened, it became extremely difficult, if not impossible, to hold my urine until an appropriate time, only one of the many benefits of ALS. This condition made for some interesting times that we were able to laugh at. After dinner one evening, the *malades* of our group and their companions were describing their experiences, as per tradition. All of a sudden, I needed to use the bathroom. By the time we were able to make a graceful exit, I was having a crisis.

We raced for the bathroom. Reaching the lobby bathrooms, we noticed through the semi-opaque door that the men's bathroom was full. Afraid that I would wet my pants, we used the vacant women's bathroom which also had a glass door. By the time Tim got me out of my wheelchair and my pants down, I urinated pretty much all over the bathroom. We could not stop laughing. It was quite a spectacle. The laughing continued with Tim on his hands and knees cleaning up the mess. He was a good sport to say the least. Aware that those in the lobby had a view of us through the glass door, we laughed even harder. In fact, soon after our pilgrimage with my weakening diaphragm, I lost my ability to laugh making this memory all the sweeter.

Despite these difficulties, the pilgrimage to Lourdes was a wonderful experience. I grew closer to God and to Our Lady. And I believe a miracle occurred, but it was not a physical miracle.

The days are filled with wonderful Mass celebrations, each in unique and historic locations. Stations of the Cross can be experienced along the Gave de Pau River across from the grotto. The able-bodied have the opportunity to experience the Stations of the Cross on the hillside above the grotto. There are two processions daily, and, of course, time is set aside for frequent visits to the grotto.

There was also a lecture for the small group of physicians from the Federal Association of the Order of Malta on the pilgrimage. We had the privilege of spending an hour with the official physician of Our Lady of Lourdes Sanctuary, François-Bernard Michel. François-Bernard Michel and his team exhaustively research all claimed miracles. The research take years and decades before officially declared a miracle. The charismatic and insightful Cardinal Timothy Dolan (an archbishop at the time) also addressed our group, "Coming to Lourdes is like coming home to mom." That statement really hit home for me.

One afternoon, the _malades_ and their companions separated to attend separate discussion groups. Following our lecture, we were given the opportunity to receive the sacrament of Reconciliation. It was cathartic, and a flood of emotions came forth emptying me. I wept for thirty minutes with Father Richard Mullins at my side consoling me.

At Lourdes, there are two processions a day: the Eucharistic Procession in the afternoon and the candlelit Possession of the Holy Rosary in the evening. Each procession starts at the grotto and winds through the Sanctuary of Our Lady of Lourdes. Most of the _malades_ were transported on three-wheeled carts, some on beds. I was uneasy at the prospect of spending the day in the cart which had little back and no head support. But as it turns out, the discomfort was minimal, and though Tim brought along my ventilator, I surprisingly didn't need it.

The Eucharistic Procession culminates in the Basilica of Pope Pius X, and 20,000 of us packed into the Basilica for an Adoration service after the procession. Hundreds of us _malades_ lined up side-by-side surrounding the altar. It was both comforting and powerful to be there with Christ and among so many sick people from all over the world. Several members of the Order continually distributed water from the sacred spring to us. It is hard for me to describe the emotions and the joy.

The Procession of the Holy Rosary begins at dusk, again starting at the grotto and winding along the Gave de Pau River and through the Domain. This candlelit procession ends in the breathtaking square in front of the Basilica of the Holy Rosary. There were thousands of us *malades*, companions, volunteers, and members of the Order of Malta, each holding a lit candle and singing the *Ave Maria* in alternating languages. It felt like Heaven fell from the sky and gently embraced us.

In the evenings, after a long day, we found ourselves drawn back to the grotto to pray and be with Our Lady of Lourdes. We would sit at the grotto in awe while being nourished by the spring water. The serenity was like nothing I have ever felt before.

No rock concert or sporting event could ever deliver this feeling. Still energized, we sometimes enjoyed a few spirits back at the hotel lounge before retiring for the night. Tim, Chuck and I cherished the opportunity to bond with and hear the stories of other pilgrims.

One brisk rainy morning, Tim and I along with hundreds of others from all over the world were submerged in the sacred spring water. While we were submerged, we said a brief prayer and kissed a statue of the Blessed Virgin Mary. The experience was so moving that we both were submerged in the 60°C sacred spring water again a few days later.

I told Chuck and Tim, about how my daughter Cecilia, twelve-years-old at the time, would not let me read to her or do homework with her until I got better. She also made me promise that if I went to Lourdes that I would get better. She was bargaining, part of the normal grieving process. But somehow, it did not feel right to pray for physical healing, as much as I wanted it, especially for my family's sake. Why would I deserve that, I thought, knowing full well of all the suffering in the world? Even more so, He had already shown mercy on my life. All of my prayers as a thirteen-year-old boy had been answered.

Instead, I prayed for my family. I prayed for the graces to not only accept this illness with dignity, but to somehow turn ALS into a positive for my family and friends. I prayed for healing of soul rather than of body, and I feel a miracle did happen that week in Lourdes.

CHAPTER NINE

PHYSICAL DETERIORATION AND SPIRITUAL REHABILITATION

The most potent and acceptable prayer is the prayer that leaves the best effects. I don't mean it must immediately fill the soul with desire. . . . The best effects [are] those that are followed up by actions—when the soul not only desires the honor of God, but really strives for it.

—St. Teresa of Avila

I am so grateful that I was able to make the pilgrimage with two great friends. This pilgrimage changed me to the core. My faith was fortified changing my perspective. This experience helped me reassess my life, how I perceived others and all of nature. It brought me peace. I pray that one day my family will make the pilgrimage to the Sanctuary of Our Lady of Lourdes.

As I connect the sequence of events that led me to Our Lady of Lourdes, I can only think, Divine Providence. I submitted my application for the trip just in time. If I had hesitated at all, I would have never made the pilgrimage and missed out on all the riches it has brought to my life.

I made many new friends on my pilgrimage. I will never forget the time spent with Abbot Placid Solari sitting on the banks of the Gave de Pau River across from the grotto. I am so grateful for his counsel on the pilgrimage, and for his continued counsel today. He often offers private Masses for me and my family at Belmont Abbey and makes frequent visits to my home.

The fellowship and counsel of several Knights and Dames of Malta help sustain me to this day. My new friend, John Gannon KM, has organized weekly gatherings for Mass and lunch, which are often the highlights of my week.

Several prayers, some of them learned in Lourdes, entered my daily routine. I found myself drawn to Mother Theresa and frequently say Novenas to her. I also began praying the Rosary with frequency and meditating on its mysteries. This meditation has brought me insight into the opportunity in suffering.

My physical deterioration is limited to my motor neurons and subsequently my voluntary muscles. The rest of my body is fully functional. The problem is that our voluntary muscles give us animation and allow us to do all things physical. This means that my five senses and brain function remain otherwise intact. So I feel and often I am able to anticipate pain and discomfort without the ability to do anything about it.

Discomforts became magnified when my ability to alter my environment was lost. It can be at times frustrating and a bit scary. Ants and gnats crawl on me as if I were a corpse. At one point, I found several baby spiders crawling on me. There must have been a nest somewhere on my power chair. It is a constant test of my character. By the grace of God, the tests are getting easier.

In February 2011, I became confined to a wheelchair. Since then, all of my waking moments have been spent in that chair. There has been continuous pressure on my backside No longer able to stretch or readjust my seated position makes each day a challenge.

Fortunately, much of my day is filled with joy, which comes from focusing on my current abilities, my many blessings, and a more complete union with Christ. I am well aware that I have a long way to go. In fact, most of my joy is derived from anticipation of a complete union with Christ. Reflecting on my lost abilities enhances the joy I receive from my remaining abilities...

An old man reminiscing on a wonderful life, I am grateful for the memories. I am also thankful for the opportunity to pursue higher-level thinking, and for my remaining abilities of sight, hearing, taste, smell, and the touch, which remain and which I appreciate more now. I find joy in simple things: a hug, a conversation, a hot shower and a warm blanket. I keep a small cashmere blanket from my mother-in-law, even in the hot summer months.

ALS is different from a spinal cord injury where the dorsal and ventral nerve roots (motor and sensory nerves of the spinal cord) are affected. With the sensory nervous system intact, ALS allows for much suffering. I do not mean to imply that spinal cord injury patients do not suffer. The suddenness of their condition makes their mental anguish unfathomable.

In fact, a benefit of ALS is that the touch and embrace of a loved one makes the added pain and discomforts worthwhile. Additionally, suffering, I have found, provides an opportunity to achieve much good. I like to start each day with the Morning Offering Prayer. In the prayer, I offer up my prayers, works, joys and sufferings of each day in reparation for all of my sins and in thanks for my many talents and gifts.

When I was a child I would complain often, to which my mother responded: "Offer it up." I did not understand what she meant at the time. Throughout the years, I have had trouble understanding this. Why suffer? What good can come from it? But ALS has opened my eyes and my heart to the wonderful power of suffering. This simple act—"offer it up"—has such profound immediate and eternal consequences.

More recently, through the guidance of a friend and mentor, Jerry Schmitt, KM, I have been offering up my suffering in a specific, more meaningful way, which in turn has lessened my suffering. I simply take a specific pain, discomfort, or disappointment and offer it up to Christ for a specific person, family, group, or idea.

In addition to understanding and embracing suffering, ALS, in stripping me of pride, hobbies, and material distractions, has built me up in a way that I could not attain when healthy. Once liberated from distractions and false idols, in many ways, I became much happier. ALS, then, in many ways, has been a gift, despite its many painful consequences. ALS has given me time; time to slow down, time for meditation and prayer leading to intuitions. Old hobbies are gone, but I have new ones; namely, a fuller connection to my family, deeper meditation, more fervent prayer, better reading, and more frequent and deeper reception of the sacraments of Penance and Holy Communion. All these things were a part of my life when I was healthy, but I was only scratching the surface. In particular, I became a much more avid reader after I became confined to my wheelchair.

Preferring nonfiction, I first read the Gospels and self-help type books of encouragement given to me by family and friends following my diagnosis. However, muscle weakness rapidly progressed in my hands, and I became unable to turn a page in a book. Furthermore, the electronic version of the Bible I had on my iPad required me to swipe the screen in order to turn the page. When I lost the ability to do this and became too weak to push the buttons on my Kindle, I thought reading was a thing of the past.

I did not read for quite some time. This inability to read, lack of intellectual growth coupled with the progressive physical deterioration, led to some anxiety. Finally, my friend, Abbot Placid Solari, showed me on his iPad how he could change the page with a light touch on the corner of the screen. I was thrilled. It turns out that my electronic version of the Bible was an anomaly. I began with *Unbroken*, recommended by my good friend, Quintin Shuler.

In February 2013, Abbot Placid Solari brought me to a Charlotte Catholic men's conference. We joined a group of more than eight hundred, and the Abbott heard confessions most of the day while I attended lectures.

While I was waiting to receive the sacrament of Reconciliation, a man behind me noticed my smart phone mounted on my wheelchair. He told me of "Truth and Life," an app headed by Cardinal George of the Chicago diocese. The app gives you access to a dramatized version of the Bible, Zenit, updated sermons, articles, blogs, and videos. He said it would be easy for me to follow along on my iPhone. While the audio plays, the text of the verses is highlighted on the screen. Between the automation and the dramatized narration, the Bible never had more meaning for me. Of course, I am in a different place spiritually than I was two years ago. The app has been a joy, I am most grateful to the gentleman for sharing it with me.

Friends Grattan and Julie Brown introduced me to Thomas Merton's, *The Seven Story Mountain* and Michael Novak's work. I read several of his books including, *Three in One*. In this book, Mr. Novak rekindled a passion in me for economics, my college major. I was reminded of the yearning I had in helping others, prior to my illness.

CHAPTER TEN

AIR HUNGER AND OTHER PLEASANTRIES

Do everything calmly and peacefully. Do as much as you can as well as you can. Strive to see God in all things without exception, and consent to His will joyously. Do everything for God, uniting yourself to him in word and deed. Walk very simply with the Cross of the Lord and be at peace with yourself.
                                                    —St. Francis de Sales

I have no reserve capacity of strength to my few remaining, weakened voluntary muscles, which makes me vulnerable. A crisis is only a moment away. If the mouthpiece on my ventilator is slightly out of place, my lips quickly fatigue and I cannot purse my lips to form a seal around the mouth piece. If my hand slips from the drive control on my wheelchair, it may be too late before someone finds me.

The inevitable progression of ALS leads to continually new limitations and often unpleasant predicaments. A particularly troublesome occurrence is "air hunger." I can only breathe now via a ventilator. It is often difficult for me to eat. Chewing and swallowing are slow, sometimes I am desperate to take a breath as I try to get the bite of food down. Expressing myself verbally is clumsy and requires much patience on the part of family and friends. And I am always one slip away from the ventilator moving out of my reach and being unable to breathe.

My ventilator has literally been a lifesaver, but it can also be a nuisance. It is equipped with alarms. They were sounding off continually, through the night, and after many sleepless nights, Kirsten and I decided to have them disabled. Subsequently, nights became much more restful for both of us. One evening, however, Kirsten got me settled in bed and then went to lock up the house and straighten up the kitchen. The tubing somehow slipped from the mask and fell to the floor.

Suddenly, having the ventilator alarms shut off did not seem like such a good idea. At first, I was terrified. My weakened voice was muffled by the ventilator mask. I began to sweat. I could see myself in the mirror and thought, so this is how it will end for me. I closed my eyes and began to pray. It was not long before I was calm and at peace. To my surprise, a ventilator alarm sounded. It was set to not go off for five minutes. Kirsten rushed in and fixed the problem. We then set the alarm to a one-minute delay. If I went five minutes today, I would die.

Mid April 2013, spring was in full bloom and I was enjoying a warm sunny morning on my front porch listening to birds sing while various bees and insects flew about me. Kirsten was planting flowers in front of the house near me. I was filled with joy and peace. I was deeply happy. A hornet came, however, and spoiled my fun. I decided it would be best to go into the house. As I crossed the threshold, my head lurched forward and pushed my ventilator out of reach.

I fairly calmly searched the house for Kirsten. My calm, however, quickly turned to panic when I saw her planting flowers in our courtyard. Now sweating, I turned my wheelchair around, briefly getting stuck in a doorway. I backed my wheelchair up into the courtyard door in hopes that she would hear me. The last thing I remember was moving my wheelchair forward from the door so that she had room to open it if she heard me. Fortunately, she did. This event spurred us to get an alarm for me to sound in an emergency.

Aspirations are happening with increased frequency. Aspirations occur during my morning smoothie, at the dinner table, when I am having my teeth brushed, traveling in my van and in conversation on my own saliva. When this happens, my eyes water and my nose runs. Oh yeah, and I go into laryngospasm and bronchospasm. This is when my airway narrows and I cannot move air, even with the ventilator. My background and my now-extensive experience tell me that the spasm is only temporary and I will soon be able to breathe.

Mother's Day brunch 2013, we were enjoying a wonderful meal following Sunday Mass. Conversation and food consumption are not a good combination for me. I distinctly remember enjoying a bite of lamb when I decided it would be a good idea to talk. Well, the lamb ended up in my airway precipitating the tears and laryngospasm. Kirsten wiped my tears and nose while I patiently waited to take a breath. The rest of the meal was uneventful. It was a beautiful and memorable day. A machine that helps me cough and clear my airways revealed the culprit when we got home.

One afternoon, before I became confined to my wheelchair, Kirsten and I were going out to lunch and running some errands before we picked up our children from school. Kirsten ran out to the barn to check on the horses. I was unable to stand up straight and needed a cane to assist me while walking short distances. I remember reaching down to pick up a piece of garbage in the driveway when I lost my balance and fell over. I did not injure myself, but that part of the driveway was sloped and I fell with my head below my feet. At the time, I needed a ventilator whenever I laid flat. Lying in this position made breathing even more labored.

I was too weak to reach for my phone to call my wife and I could not muster up enough wind to yell for help. I was concerned that I would not make it before she came back. A five-minute trip to the barn often meant twenty minutes or more. Fortunately, two kind men renovating our bathroom to make it handicap accessible, appeared from the house before the situation got too serious. They helped me to my car; I thanked them and reassured them that I was in good shape. Kirsten soon arrived and we had a pleasant afternoon together, like nothing had happened, except that I had a new respect for gravity.

It was this event that convinced me that it was no longer safe for me to walk. It was not long before I remained in my wheelchair when I was not in bed.

There have been several falls. It took a few falls before Kirsten came to the realization that she could no longer manually transfer me. We began using the Hoyer lift that had been in our bedroom for a few months. A Hoyer lift is a machine that transfers me in a sling between my bed, power wheelchair, and shower chair. Eventually, the burden would be too much, and I would need a caregiver.

It would take some time for Kirsten to relinquished duties of toileting, bathing and dressing. Frankly, it was hard for me as well, but I knew that she needed help. Stress in our relationship would build prior to each transition, with Kirsten fighting each change as it was a reminder of my inevitable demise. After each transition was made, we would experience a renewed peace and joy.

Interestingly, I welcomed transitions every step of the way. I was relieved and grateful that there were technologies and resources available to relieve my suffering. But also, satisfied with the last, I welcomed each new chapter of my life. I laid it all at the feet of Christ.

In May 2011, Kirsten and our daughter, Cecilia, went to Pinehurst, North Carolina, for a horse show Cecilia was competing in. I was home with our two boys. Personal hygiene was becoming progressively more challenging but I was able to struggle through it. We put a bench in the shower as I could not stand for long without fatigue or losing my balance. Kirsten had William, nine years old at the time, sit in the bathroom in case I needed help while I showered.

This particular time was a struggle. I asked William if he minded helping me wash. He jumped at the opportunity, concealing well any embarrassment. I believe that he was more concerned that I might be humiliated by the situation. William has always been perceptive of other people's feelings and eager to assist me. He frequently asks to be my caregiver and assists me day in and day out with much of my care.

That was the last horse show Kirsten would attend with Cecilia without me. The following year 2012, Cecilia was ranked in the top ten, several times number one, in the country for large pony hunter. It was an exciting year for Cecilia and all of us. Sadly, Kirsten and I had to miss most of her shows due to my illness and the activities of Cecilia's younger brothers. We could no longer divide and conquer the responsibilities. We are grateful to Cecilia's grandmother Kathy who flew in from Chicago to accompany Cecilia at her horse shows. We could not have done it and certainly would not have had the success without her generous help.

Many things did not go right today and I still struggle with emailing and texting family and friends. Siri is increasingly having trouble recognizing my voice and I am having more trouble making corrections. My arms now can only move my motionless hands a few inches. A brace supports my wrist allowing my thumb to reach most of the keys on my phone. This movement is short lived for soon the atrophied residual motor neurons and muscles are fatigued. I rest and take a break until the energy returns. This situation is my reality and I am perfectly fine with it, mostly. This is my cross, a cross that is only getting heavier.

Despite all this, I feel a deep connection with everything. Upon saying my morning prayers June 25, 2013, a joy came over me like I had never experienced before. My insides were warm and dancing with energy, I was euphoric. I had experienced something like this before, but never to this extent and duration. For two days, I was overwhelmed with positive vibes, bursting with energy.

The intense euphoria was briefly interrupted on June 27, 2013. My caregiver got me started on my passive exercise bike, which moves my legs for me. My floppy paralyzed feet need to be strapped to the pedals as they would otherwise slip off. After positioning me and setting up the exercise bike she walked into the kitchen. She did not notice that my ventilator mouthpiece was up by my forehead out of my reach. I clicked with my tongue as there was no air in my lungs to speak.

When I heard the door to the house close, I thought I was alone and started to panic. My seventy-seven-year-old father was in for a visit, I heard his shuffling feet and was hopeful that he would come and adjust my mouthpiece. He had never done this before and was not used to being my caregiver. He is also hard of hearing and could not hear my desperate clicking. My heart began to pound in my chest.

Locked into the exercise bike I drove my wheelchair backwards dragging the bike into the kitchen doorway. My dad asked me if I wanted a piece of chocolate. He could only see the side of my face from the way I was positioned in the doorway. It did not occur to him that I was positioned awkwardly in my chair with the exercise bike still cycling my legs. He actually held up a piece of chocolate to my face in my desperation. In this moment of agony I had, of all things, a comic flash, thinking this would make for rich Saturday Night Live material.

The comic flash turned on an instant to fear when I noticed my heart rhythm change. My father eventually became aware of my condition. He grabbed my slumped head and put the mouthpiece in my mouth. He was shaken and felt awful that he did not notice the situation sooner. It was ten minutes before I felt better.

These cycles of intense joy and intense suffering have replaced my past cycles of hard work and hedonism, and I am better for it.

CHAPTER ELEVEN

DAYS AND NIGHTS WITH ALS

The more you try to avoid suffering, the more you suffer, because smaller and more insignificant things begin to torture you, in proportion to your fear of being hurt. The one who does most to avoid suffering is, in the end, the one who suffers most.
—Thomas Merton

I was seven years-old when my tonsils were removed. I still remember the distress that I caused the nurses when they tried to start an IV. Following the procedure, I was on a liquid diet. I remember the taste of the chicken broth like it was yesterday. It is funny how the mind works, thoughts of that soup still make me salivate. My taste buds must have been out of sorts, it had been a day or so since my last meal. When I asked my mom if she could make me this soup when we got home from the hospital, she laughed. It was chicken bullion.

Through my ventilator mask, I can see my wife's smiling face holding a hot cup of coffee. Its morning and relief is on the way. Kirsten sets her coffee next to my ventilator, the aroma fills my mask. This is the only way I can smell. The only time air passes through my nose. When I am up in my wheelchair, my ventilator fills my lungs through a mouthpiece, bypassing my olfactory nerve. She takes off my soft boots that protect me from getting pressure sores and begins giving range of motion to my feet and ankles. The pain is soon gone. She then slides a sling behind my back and under my legs and transfers me from my bed to my power wheelchair with the Hoyer lift. The ventilator mask is removed and I am greeted with a sip of delicious coffee. It truly is the little things in life, a smile and a cup of coffee.

The night was rough. They all have been rough lately. I have been unable to move in bed for two years now. The pain in my backside has been getting worse over the past several weeks. I now have to wake up Kirsten a few times a night to reposition me. The night before we were optimistic, an air cushioned mattress pad arrived. After waking up twice in the middle of the night with severe tailbone pain, my wife gave me a pain pill and transferred me into my power chair. That is where I awoke the next morning.

Bad days and moments are often followed by great and beautiful days and moments. I believe that this is a metaphor for life. God is showing us that suffering and death can be healing and beautiful. All suffering which can seem overwhelming is nothing compared to the glory of God. In dying we are born into eternal life. Death brings new life, hopefully in Heaven.

Following intense pain, when it is relieved, there is a period of euphoria. Following a period of frustration or disappointment comes peace, a calm always follows a storm. I am reminded of the time our son Jack had an encounter with a stingray while swimming on Kiawah Island. Kirsten said that he screamed in pain the entire forty-minute trip to a medical clinic in Charleston. As soon as the pain was relieved, Jack was elated. Kirsten had never seen him so up. What was once mundane to him became joyful. We were struck by his intense euphoria which lasted into the evening.

ALS brings much suffering, pain, frustration, and disappointment but not without euphoria and peace. During times of trial, great and small, it is important to remember that the suffering will end; peace and joy are around the corner. Similarly, when everything seems to be right in our lives, it is important to remember the suffering of others.

***   ***   ***

I roll out to the kitchen where I meet our children having breakfast and getting their things together for school. Jack, my youngest, often gives me my morning medication with water. He is always the first one ready and cheerfully does many of the morning chores. I can only imagine how hard it is on Kirsten, Cecilia, William and Jack. They are all handling this rollercoaster of emotions so beautifully. I am immensely proud of each of them.

Kirsten now drives our children to school while I stay home either with a caregiver or by myself. It has become too difficult to get me ready, load me in the van and still get our children to school on time. I take this quiet time to finish up my prayers, catch up on email, or read. If my wife does not have to go to work, we have breakfast together. Then she or my caregiver helps me get cleaned up for the day. Most days, they give me range-of-motion exercises and sometimes I get hooked up to my passive exercise bike. The movement helps reduce pain and maintains flexibility which helps them out when they dress me.

On the days my wife works, we often meet for lunch and then I do errands with my caregiver. There is a little time to read and then it is time to pick up our children from school. Late afternoons and evenings are always busy with snacks, homework, violin, piano, equestrian lessons and depending on the season, soccer, basketball, cross-country, swimming and golf.

We have dinner together most evenings thanks to Kirsten's cooking. She is a wonderful cook. Often we read together, do homework, practice violin and piano. Occasionally, if there is time, we watch part of a ball game. Then hugs and kisses goodnight. My wife tucks our children into bed upstairs. It has been two years since I have been upstairs to tuck them in. That was always my job, my favorite part of the day. We enjoyed silly time, reading, talking about their day, songs, tickling and prayers. The nightly routine was an hour or more.

My nighttime routine is difficult for Kirsten when we do not have a caregiver. She is understandably exhausted from triple duty as a parent, physician and caring for me. We are emotionally and physically exhausted. Getting me cleaned up and positioned comfortably in bed, night after night, is a laborious process. Kirsten has been doing this for more than two years. However, her stress and suffering has led us to get our children more involved in my care. This simple decision to let our children be more involved in my care has strengthened our appreciation of one another.

Once a week, I look forward to meeting with friends, members of the Order of Malta, I made on my pilgrimage to Lourdes, France. We celebrate a weekday Mass together before we go out for lunch. Traveling to Charlotte for weekday Mass, I had a sudden urge to urinate. Stuck at a stoplight, I prayed that I could hold it until my caregiver could pull over to help.

I ended up urinating on myself, my power chair and the van floor before she could assist me. Nevertheless, McKenzie cleaned up my chair the best she could and we went on to enjoy a wonderful Mass. It was April 16, 2013, the day after the Boston Marathon bombing and I was determined to receive the Mass. Soaked with urine, I did excuse myself from our lunch date.

Interpreting nuclear medicine studies was part of my practice as a radiologist. The radioisotope is often secreted in the urine. We were frequently puzzled by urine contamination in remote parts of the body. As I think about my naïveté, I have to laugh. I have urinated on myself at basketball practices, soccer games, shopping centers, violin recitals, in my van, in my home and in my bed. Although I urinated on myself enroute to Mass despite my prayer, I stayed calm and was able to achieve and enjoy most of what I wanted to that day.

A few years ago, my ninety-six-year-old grandmother Dolores Marie Hansen, told me that every seven years we enter a new phase of our life. I had never heard this before, but it made a lot of sense. An adolescent is no longer interested in the things of a toddler, the teen interested in that of an adolescent and so on. Today, the simple things bring me joy: Talking to loved ones, celebrating Mass, prayer, the taste of foods, a glass of wine or cup of coffee. Receiving range of motion on my arms and legs is my exercise. This simple act, although passive suffices as my exercise, my hike, my tennis match and my round of golf.

Soon, my ability to speak and eat will pass. But, I will have my memory, wonderful memories and I thank God for that. Once fearful of having cognitive function in my deterioration, I now see it as a blessing. The sight, sound and touch of a loved one, sunshine, rain, a blossom bring overwhelming joy. Just as the chicken bullion was intensely satisfying after my tonsillectomy, I will be happy, joyous.

CHAPTER TWELVE

ALEA IACTA EST

I might have been given a bad break, but I've got an awful lot to live for.
—Lou Gehrig

The idiom "Crossing the Rubicon" means to pass a point of no return. The Rubicon is a river in northern Italy. After much consternation, Julius Caesar led his legion of troops across the Rubicon in January of the year 49 BC. Crossing the river would be a clear sign of insurrection, showing Pompey and the rest of the leaders of the Roman Republic, that Caesar meant to wrest power from them. Before crossing the Rubicon, Julius Caesar was perplexed and carefully contemplated his options. At the river's edge, feeling the full weight of his decision, he quoted his favorite poet Menander *"alea iacta est"*—"the die is cast."

Not long before I retired on disability, a colleague of mine, Robert Miller, told me about an article that discussed how in the not-too-distant future, all of the information stored in our brains, memories, ideas, etc., could be downloaded into a computer. The silicone chip could exist long after our physical bodies have perished, a virtual self. I did not realize at the time, that I would become that silicone chip. All of my memories, ideas, sense of humor and love preserved, locked within motionless otherwise living tissue.

Unfortunately, advancements in technology have raised an ethical dilemma. ALS patients and their families have to decide whether to initiate ventilatory support on top of the other endless needs. The tremendous cost of caregivers and sacrifice of time and emotion, must be weighed against the benefit of having the patient linger lucidly within a corpse.

If the ALS patient lives long enough, there is an existence when all voluntary movement is lost. The patient becomes "locked in" with no ability to communicate. The ability to express love, joy, encouragement, pain and despair are lost. This "locked in" state is a scary proposition both for the patient and for the patient's family.

Fortunately, the progression of voluntary muscle loss is not sudden or acute. It stands to reason, that if the patient was approaching this "locked in" state, they could communicate their will using eye gaze technology. The extraocular muscles, giving us eye movement, are usually a last to go. If the patient is not fortunate enough to die as a result of a complication of ALS, such as a fall, pneumonia, pulmonary embolus or inadvertent suffocation, he, or worse yet a loved one, will have to make a most unnatural decision. They will have to make a decision to end a life.

From the outside I am gaining on a comatose appearance, all but dead, meanwhile my five senses and my mind are as sharp as ever. Despite my physical and emotional suffering, most of the time, I derive great joy from my existence.

That said, many ALS patients become passive and take on the role of victim squandering precious remaining time. Depression runs rampant in ALS families. Just 21 percent of ALS patients pursue noninvasive (face mask) ventilators let alone invasive (tracheostomy) ones. A recent study found that many do this for financial reasons. The astronomical costs of caregivers, medicine and equipment quickly exhaust the life savings of all but the wealthiest patients. Therefore, caregiving is frequently left up to family and friends. Sadly, most lack an adequate support system and care suffers. It is difficult enough to endure the physical and emotional suffering in the best of circumstances. The ALS patient too often loses sight of any value in their existence and chooses to end their life rather than burden their families.

In fact, the death of the ALS patient has become, more often than not, a conscious decision made by man. When the patient has had enough, they simply notify their physician or social worker who then initiates hospice care. The hospice caregiver initiates intravenous morphine, and if the patient is ventilator dependent, the dirty deed is done in a matter of minutes. If he or she is not ventilator dependent, it could take a few days. The suffering is over, the opportunity is over.

At first glance, this reality is repugnant. Yet, the sad fact is that most ALS patients leave this world in this way. Depression and despair are pervasive. The only way to embrace this disease or any life for that matter is through surrender and faith. Surrender all one's abilities and possessions to the Lord. Thank you, forgive me and Thy will be done brings fulfillment and joy to any trial or tribulation. I often reflect on this beautiful line from St. Teresa of Avila: "We can only learn to know ourselves and do what we can—namely, surrender our will and fulfill God's will in us."

Our King Charles Cavalier spaniel, Fenwick, was put down recently. By the end, he could not walk on his own and he lost interest in eating. Many tears were shed, but we felt like we were doing the right thing. Most of us believe that human beings are different than our canine friends. We believe that there is a spiritual, sacred and eternal element that dogs may not have. All life is sacred, but human beings were made in God's image and likeness. We live differently than animals and I believe we should die differently.

I don't want to be euthanized. Even in my state, I feel I have purpose and He has a purpose for me. Additionally, life now is fulfilling like never before. Given this surprising reality, why would life with a tracheostomy be any different? Giving up the spoken word in light of all the other lost abilities...life will remain wonderful.

I am incredibly grateful for the numerous quality-of-life-maintaining and life-sustaining technologies that are available to me. I am well aware of the hundreds of thousands of past ALS patients who have not had, and those who do not have even today, the access to these advantages that I rely on. Lou Gehrig, the New York Yankee great, gave his famous farewell speech on July 4, 1939 and died on June 2, 1941 just two years after he first became symptomatic. Forrest Bird would not invent the ventilator for another thirteen years. Today's ventilators are small and portable, the size of a lunch box. This life-sustaining medical technology, which is covered by medical insurance and Medicare, provides a tremendous opportunity to maintain and enhance lives and families.

When you compare the minor inconveniences of noninvasive ventilation with the alternative—death—I would argue that it is suicide not to take advantage of something as simple as noninvasive ventilation. So much opportunity lost.

As a parent of a young family, living with noninvasive ventilation was an easy decision. These past few years, while on noninvasive ventilation around the clock and enduring near-complete paralysis, have been probably the most fulfilling years of my life. What a travesty it would have been to give up without at least trying this life-sustaining medical device.

I am deeply saddened by the thousands and thousands of ALS patients that do not see any value in their existence. As a culture, we judge ourselves and each other by what we can do and how much we make. ALS has reminded me of a lesson I learned as a young man, but sometimes forgot, measure people by how they manifest love, compassion and mercy not by how much they make or what they do for living.

It is a fluid situation. I do not know what I do not know, as I am fond of saying. I like this saying because although I am continually investigating and seeking to understand, I by no means feel that I know or am even aware of all there is to know. My ignorance is waxing with my understanding.

Maybe I will be miserable. Perhaps my suffering will become too great to bear. Although, I might be perfectly content and even joyous.

I am a fighter and I love a challenge. As long as my loved ones are benefiting from my existence, I am leaning towards getting a tracheostomy tube. If I happen to survive reaching the "locked in" state, however, I will have advanced directives to end my physical life. My mind turned off long after my voluntary body. I want to spare my family from having to make that decision.

I am reminded of the article discussing our life's memories downloaded onto a computer that my colleague shared with me. I was not intrigued by this idea at the time nor am I today. The only eternal existence I yearn for is in Heaven. At least this is where I stand today. Maybe I am not as decisive as Julius Caesar, but the die has been cast nonetheless. I do not worry, though. The Holy Spirit will guide me.

THE PARADOX OF ALS

Our mortality which seems like a distant star comes into focus with an ALS diagnosis. The introduction to our mortality is often met with fear and grief. With the proper perspective, however, our mortality can become beautiful, but we must look beyond the immediately physical.

Our minds and all of our organs remain fully functional, yet we appear as a corpse. In fact, only motor neurons are directly affected. Voluntary (skeletal) muscles wither secondarily in in ALS patients. All other tissues are uninvolved. My ninety-six-year-old grandmother's intermediate and long term memory is quite good, meanwhile her short-term memory is almost nonexistent. Our conversations cycle through the same topics over and over in the same conversation. "Can you walk?" No I have not walked for two and a half years. "I can still walk but I have to use my walker, it has a nice basket." "Are you able to drive?" No, I have not driven for a few years. "Oh, well at least you can still walk."

This series of questions is repeated several times with wonderful stories of my childhood intermingled. She seems to enjoy her quality of life even though she never leaves her apartment and moves about her apartment on a very limited basis. She has had several falls and compression fractures involving all the vertebrae of her spine. She is visited once a day by her son and/or daughter-in-law and rarely has any other visitors. All of her friends and contemporaries have passed away.

Although I am completely dependent on others, I consider my quality of life vastly superior to my grandmother's. I am living with my wife and children and continue to play an active role in their lives. I am able to keep up with family and friends. I get out of the house just about every day and still very much enjoy my life.

No one would consider euthanizing my grandmother with her failing mind and body. Yet, every day completely functional ALS patients with the exception of voluntary muscle loss are being silently euthanized. Of course it is not called euthanasia because the morphine doesn't directly bring about death they say. Turning off the ventilator brings about death is the argument. If the patient does not need a ventilator to breathe, the morphine will slow respiration leading to organ failure and death in a manner of a day or so.

Although we cannot move, and many of us cannot breathe on our own, we have the ability to contribute to our families and communities. With insufficient finances or available care, many lose sight of the value of their existence as society has lost sight of any value in them.

I don't think anyone would argue that the poor, sick, and elderly are not underserved. Meanwhile we have a record number of people out of work. We have countless people that need work, supply, and countless people that need care, demand. Yet, we have no plan of action to remedy this dual tragedy, matching the supply of the unemployed and underemployed workforce with the need for care.

We spend billions on unemployment benefits while the sick, poor and elderly are underserved. Precious time and talent wasted on cable TV and cell phones without an opportunity for compassionate care building self-esteem for all individuals involved. Both, those providing care and those receiving it will benefit materially and even more importantly, they will each benefit on a humanistic level.

The dirty little secret of ALS is that the demise of the patient in the large majority of cases is not pneumonia, a fall, or a blood clot, but rather a defeated spirit; a spirit that sees no value in his existence, only a burden on family, friends, and society. This is why it is so important to create and maintain meaning in life through faith and contact with loved ones. One of the biggest obstacles to this is access to daily care for the patient's continual and progressive needs.

If we as a nation dedicated resources to train some of the unemployed to deliver compassionate care to the vulnerable of our society, the goodwill will be contagious. Certainly those lives directly involved will be changed. But, I believe this paradigm shift will positively impact all of society. Generations and cultures will be brought together, bonds will be made, gratitude and goodwill will prevail.

I have decided to embrace each new chapter of my life until it's natural end. This decision has brought immense enjoyment and has minimized the suffering. To some, the line of a natural end has been blurred by technologies, in my case a ventilator. My new vision has brought this blurred line into razor sharp focus, on the other side of assisted ventilation. As long as the mind is functioning, ventilation should be encouraged. Just as the light bulb, telephone, automobile, airplane and computer have enhanced our lives, so too has the ventilator enhanced the lives of ALS patients and so many others

CHAPTER THIRTEEN
MANAGING FEAR WITH FAITH
AND PRAYER

Our deepest fear is not that we are inadequate.
Our deepest fear is that we are powerful beyond measure.
It is our light, not our darkness
That most frightens us.
We ask ourselves
Who am I to be brilliant, gorgeous, talented, fabulous?
Actually, who are you not to be?
You are a child of God.
Your playing small
Does not serve the world.
There's nothing enlightened about shrinking
So that other people won't feel insecure around you.
We are all meant to shine,
As children do.
We were born to make manifest
The glory of God that is within us.
It's not just in some of us;
It's in everyone.
And as we let our own light shine,
We unconsciously give other people permission to do the same.
As we're liberated from our own fear,
Our presence automatically liberates others.
—Marianne Williamson, "Our Deepest Fear"

During those first few months after my diagnosis, I was scared. Often, I cried myself to sleep. I would pray, "Thank you, forgive me and Thy will be done". It wasn't long, a matter of weeks, and the fear was gone. My prayers, on my pilgrimage to Lourdes and since, have evolved. Prayer now frequently involves ideas, imagery, and emotions. Prayer is more deeply experienced, which has helped me receive, to some extent, the gifts of the Holy Spirit: Wisdom, understanding, counsel, fortitude, knowledge, piety and fear of the Lord. I am certainly work in progress, but I work.

These gifts of the Holy Spirit have led to a wonderful healing. Knowledge, has given me a glimpse of life through God's lens in seeing my situation, in a limited way, as He does. The gift of knowledge has allowed me to determine His purpose for my life. The gift of piety gives me the desire to worship God out of love and not out of duty. I have transitioned from being at the Mass, a time for meditation and an obligation to check off my to-do list, to being *in* the Mass. Mass was often a chore, interfering with my free time, now it is not long enough.

I pray for all those I have sinned against throughout my life, and I try to think of specific examples. I forgive myself, realizing that this only has any meaning if I am truly sorry. I have found that forgiving those that have wronged me and loved ones and praying for their well-being, physical and spiritual, brings a peace and joy within me. This is particularly powerful, an immediate mood elevator. I pray for all suffering in the world, past, present and future. Obviously, I continually pray for my loved ones, that their lives will be enriched by my illness. I pray for the graces to handle my physical and emotional suffering in a way that brings this to fruition. Ownership of this responsibility is mine.

For a long time, I feared if and how I would be remembered. When I was able to rein in these fears, and it was not easy, life got easier. Fears now in the foreground of my mind are failing as a husband, father, brother, friend and Christian. I fear alienating myself from God, out of love for Him. These fears right me when I get off course. I always had these fears but sometimes they were pushed to the background of my consciousness by work, sport, or material possessions and desires.

I now realize that living a moral life and contributing to the moral cultural society is all that matters. The gift of wisdom has helped me order my relationship with the material world. When I get discouraged or disappointed, myopic in my thoughts; I look down upon my life or my situation, from 30,000 feet. Focusing on the big picture of life gives me clarity. Knowledge, the fifth gift of the Holy Spirit, helps me see my life as He does: I am to be a humble servant. I wish that I had this clarity and the character to make good on it when I was healthy.

I am living proof that we can achieve more than expectations, both our own and that of others. Even so, my restlessness was that I felt I was not living up to my potential. Although from the outside, my life seemed nearly perfect, God was calling me to go deeper. But, I was distracted. The blessing of ALS, however, has been that it wipes away all those material distractions.

My clarity, as I was losing my abilities at work, knowing each procedure might be my last, parallels my present clarity as my oral and laryngeal spasms progress and dysarthria ensues; knowing too well that my verbal words are numbered. Meanwhile, aspiration episodes, where I choke on foods, beverages and my own saliva are happening with increased frequency; a constant reminder that each meal could be my last.

It can be scary, but I am confident that I will be given the graces to handle the sufferings and limitations that come my way. I rode in my wheelchair along with my family through the Korean, Vietnam and World War II Memorials in Washington, DC, last fall and I tried to imagine all of the suffering of those killed in action, those injured, POWs, survivors and families. It is hard to feel sorry for myself. How could I pray for a cure for my illness in light of praying for my salvation, that of my loved ones, all that are, all that ever were and all that ever will be? Although, I cannot help but feel sorry for my wife and children.

I had a vivid dream recently that was as simple as it was beautiful. It was as though the purpose of life was unveiled to me. In that dream, it became clear that We are called to live outside ourselves. A Life preoccupied with selfish needs and desires is empty. Rather, we are called to fulfill the needs of others, spiritual as much or more than anything else. When we maintain this focus outside of ourselves in a positive and productive way, our needs are paradoxically met. When we manifest Christ's love, a love that is perfect and eternal, the reward is perfect and eternal. This is no novel concept. The only thing novel was my internalization of it.

Recently, I was reflecting on how it was that I was able to avoid the trap of self pity. How was that on my pilgrimage to Lords, I prayed for healing of soul rather than healing Of body? I was conflicted. I had Spiritual depth yet I was existing, thriving in a secular world. A closer disciple of Epicurus than Jesus Christ.

I have learned both personally and professionally that flesh is finite.

It just makes sense to pray for and prepare myself for eternity. Also, I know that if I receive healing of body without healing of soul, that I would not be any better off and possibly facing an eterrnity apart from God. It is much better for myself and for my family to pray for healing of soul.

Chapter Fourteen

My Family

Love seeks one thing only: the good of the one loved. It leaves all the other secondary effects to take care of themselves. Love, therefore, is its own reward.
—Thomas Merton

My brother Mike and I have always been deeply devoted to our families. Fulfilled by our family's happiness, it was easier to sacrifice. We both cherish time with our wives and children. To us, being at our children's games and activities, and being there to tuck them in at night are paramount. This stems from treasured memories from our childhood spent with our father. Some of our favorite memories are playing ball with our father and getting tucked in at night with a prayer. The lack of frequency of these moments, however, has driven us to overachieve in this regard, no doubt. My personal hobbies never competed with their activities, and television never competed with playtime. I always tucked my kids in at night.

But with ALS, what was unacceptable, unfathomable one day, becomes reality the next. Climbing the stairs to my children's bedrooms was becoming very difficult. In August 2010, soon after my diagnosis, friends gave us their stairwell chairlift so that I could continue my nighttime routine with my children. This generous and thoughtful gift allowed me to maintain my most cherished activity for another year. Again, I had fabulous clarity knowing these were fleeting moments.

All of life is but fleeting moments, we just do not realize it.

At first, I could continue lying in bed with my children while reading stories and saying prayers as long as I had my head and torso propped up with pillows. My respiratory muscles further weakened and we gradually moved our routine to a sofa in their playroom. The upright position relieved pressure on my diaphragm making breathing easier. Before long, I was too weak and short of breath to get around upstairs without a walker and, in the end, a wheelchair. By September 2011, I became too weak to ride the chairlift and unable to breathe without my ventilator. My children's bedrooms became off limits. It was a crushing blow. My world was shrinking further.

I have sadness for my wife and children, but I also have hope and optimism. I am sad that they will not have their husband and father to share in milestones as well as life's everyday joys. I am sad that they will not have me to share in a laugh or lean on in life's disappointments, setbacks and especially during life's inevitable tragedies. Their mentor and fan, their biggest fan, will not be there for them, but He will be there. I take great comfort in that.

My goal is in preparing my family after I am gone. I find myself squeezing a lifetime of lessons into just a few years. I have an urgency in helping them lay a moral foundation; a foundation that will make them productive, compassionate, and grateful participants in society, bringing them lasting happiness, joy and peace, not to mention eternal life. This, however, will not protect them from sad moments, disappointment and tragedy. Suffering is an intimate part of the human condition. It is my prayer that the Holy Spirit blesses them with the gift of knowledge, allowing them to see life as He does.

I only want to survive with my disabilities or be cured of ALS for my family's sake. Only if they will be better off for it. I believe ALS happened for a reason. This suffering of theirs and mine can make us better Christians, better able to do God's work. As I imagine my final moments, I have little anxiety. I just want it to go well for my family. I fervently pray for the grace of a happy death, for their sake. Thus far, I feel like this prayer has been answered—a source of my peace and joy.

Disease progression leads to a continuous stream of transitions. These transitions have been difficult for Kirsten as they are a reminder of her new reality. As soon as she makes a modification to her life, adjusting to my limitations, a new limitation arises. I found each new lost ability initially frustrating as I fought to hold on to that ability. As soon as I let go, however, I never looked back. I began to anticipate new limitations and transitions. Letting go of lost abilities led to a swelling of gratitude for my remaining abilities. Even more remarkable, each new limitation led to a greater sense of connection with life, past, present and future.

May 2010 soon after my ALS diagnosis, Kirsten and I met with a social worker as part of our introduction to the ALS clinic in Charlotte, North Carolina. We needed to discuss how and when we would reveal the disease and its realities with our children. Kirsten had many questions along with her steady flow of tears. Still in shock, many questions had no answer. There were other questions that she knew the answer to, though she hoped that her understanding of the disease as a physician was somehow wrong. The hour long discussion was a blur.

One bit of advice the social worker gave us that resonated with me for more than three years now was that I should remain the head of the household even with my waning abilities. I should continue to lead, discipline and protect just like I had always done. Kirsten is very bright and capable but she usually looked to me as we made our way along the winding and sometimes rocky path of life.

***   ***   ***

I caught her off guard when I proposed to her on December 16, 1995. The day started with surprise tickets to the matinee showing of The Nutcracker at the Arie Crown Theater in Chicago. I excused myself to the bathroom a few times to make sure the engagement ring was still in my pocket. The last time I gave Kirsten jewelry, at her medical school graduation, she felt the jewelry box in my pocket before I could present it to her. I was not going to make that mistake again. The engagement ring was loose in my pocket and I was a bit nervous, well aware of the enormity of the day. I had told Kirsten that my sister Michelle and her family had invited us to dinner that evening. The cemetery where my mom was laid to rest was right on the way out to their home. I asked if she minded if we stopped so I could drop off some flowers at her grave site.

We arrived at Mary Queen of Heaven Cemetery just as the entrance gates were being locked up. Kirsten knew how important my mom was to me, she suggested that we come back the following day. I gave her a nervous smile and left her in the car while I walked over to the men locking up the gate. I offered the men $60, all of the money I had at the time. I explained to them that I brought my girlfriend out to propose to her at my mom's grave site. I really did not think the men would acquiesce but I was desperate. You cannot imagine the relief I felt when they agreed to let us come in. I was touched when the workers refused to take my money and told me to take my time. Who says prayers do not really work?

As we drove across the cemetery, Kirsten still had no idea of my plans. We walked up to the angel on my mom's headstone. I got down on one knee holding a dozen pink roses in one hand and Kirsten's hand in the other. I told her that I wanted my mom to be here in this moment. I then said that I love her and wanted to spend the rest of my life with her. I took out the engagement ring and asked if she would marry me. Her tears started as soon as I got down on one knee. It was one of the most beautiful moments of my life. The cemetery workers were waiting for us at the gate. When we pulled up to them they asked if she said yes, with a big smile I said yes.

It was then that I told Kirsten that we had dinner reservations at Charlie Trotter's Restaurant. Dinner at my sisters was just a ploy to get her to the cemetery without suspicion. Jacked with adrenaline, the trip back to the city in my old Mazda was unforgettable. I traded in my jeep for her engagement ring. The anxiety building up to the proposal was now behind us and we had a wonderful evening talking about our hopes and dreams for our future together as one. From that moment, each of our lives would change course. We aligned our sails as one ship making our way through the open seas of life.

A few of my best friends from medical school had planned to return to Chicago that weekend. We made plans to meet up at Goose Island Brewery after dinner. It turns out that it was not an accidental reunion for Ed Perez. Ed flew back from Portland, Oregon where he was doing his orthopedic surgery residency to propose to his long-time girlfriend Zoe. In fact, he proposed to her in the Goose Island parking lot moments prior to our arrival. I did not tell them of my plans, it was a most unlikely and memorable night. This was 1995, before cell phones were commonplace. The four of us made frequent trips to the only payphone calling family and friends.

A few years later, I gave her the confidence that we could bring a child into the world while we were still residents. When we found out Kirsten was pregnant, realizing that I was now responsible for a new life, I became incredibly focused on my studies and my career. Cecilia was born six weeks prior to my radiology and physics boards. After she was born, I found it extremely challenging to spend time away from them. Besides, I spent nine months studying, nesting my career, and felt confident with the material. I would not be disappointed with my board scores. For the first time, my life had meaning, I found genuine purpose.

Our engagement, marriage and births of our three children gleam as the brightest moments of my life. That is, until now. The brightest most rewarding time in my life is right now. With all of my physical suffering and lost abilities, I sit here virtually paralyzed in my chair and I am at peace and joyful.

I am not always at peace. I am not naïve enough to believe that uninterrupted peace is possible in this life. As my physical condition progressively declines, this mandate to maintain my leadership, discipline, and protection of my family has become increasingly difficult. I sometimes feel an urgency to share a lifetime of lessons and provide a lifetime of leadership, discipline and protection which can be annoying, no doubt.

   I now realize that my wife and children will be okay. The leadership and protection they needed and I gladly provided is now being fulfilled by Kirsten's capable hands. Besides, He will always be there for them and they have learned to ask through faith and persistent prayer. I can now let go. In my weakness, I have found strength.

CHAPTER FIFTEEN

MY CROSS, MY OPPORTUNITY

Suffering is a great favor. Remember that everything soon comes to an end . . .
and take courage. Think of how our gain is eternal.
                                            —St. Teresa of Avila

ALS is a slow but steady death as it marches unrelenting through my body. The mind is sharp, fully aware as the body slowly fails, choking and struggling to breathe. Moreover, I am fully aware of the stress and burden placed on loved ones. However, when I consider all the potential benefits, dying from ALS is much better than the sudden acuteness of an automobile accident, heart attack, or stroke. ALS leaves time, moments, gifts . . . opportunites.

My suffering comes on many fronts as is true for most. Least of my concern is the physical suffering, nuances of being paralyzed like not being able to scratch an itch. I have had an irritating and often painful rash on my face and scalp for well over a year now. ALS patients often become hypersensitive to tactile sensation. I am unable to adjust myself when uncomfortable. Able bodied people are constantly adjusting themselves throughout the day and night. These adjustments are usually subconscious, stretching, changing position, scratching an itch or rubbing an area of discomfort. I cannot protect myself from insects or the sun, shed clothing or covers when too warm or bundle up when cold.

I am forever at the mercy of others. I am unable to eat and drink how I want, when I want, and at the pace I want. Once fulfilled by fulfilling the needs of my loved ones, my needs now compete with theirs. It must be awful for them. Previously it was I who rushed others, annoyed with obstacles and inconvenience. Now I often feel rushed and like an inconvenience. The awareness of the burden I am putting on them and the lost satisfaction of fulfilling their needs weighs heavy on me at times. In the end, we will all be better off for it, I pray.

I am unable to put myself to bed when I am tired and get up in the morning when I am rested. I awaken each morning with the ventilator mask irritating my face and scalp. Sometimes, my feet hurt and I am overheated. This is when I say the Morning Offering Prayer, while I wait to be transferred to my wheelchair and greet my family.

Dependence on others to maintain personal hygiene and toileting is humbling and usually results in diminished hygiene in an effort to save time and minimize the inconvenience on others. Previously mindless activities that took up only moments, now take all of my concentration and energy and consume much of my day and that of others.

The debilitating cramps throughout my body have waned with my deteriorating muscles and ensuing near total paralysis. In the evening, I experience aches all over my body as a result of being unable to stretch and move on my own. I am now experiencing cramps in my jaw, throat, and tongue foreshadowing impending loss of my ability to talk and eat.

The lack of physical exercise, which I treasured so, is a source of suffering. I miss my lost abilities, least of these are the lost hobbies: golf, tennis, hiking, boating and snow skiing. I miss taking care of our farm, horses and dogs. I miss the enjoyment of the activities, but mostly I miss the time shared with family and friends.

I miss embracing friends, greeting them with a big smile and a kind word or sarcasm. I miss entertaining and socializing. Outgoing and lighthearted, I would look forward to social occasions, being silly and laughing. My respiratory muscles have severely weakened making socializing difficult and filled with awkward pauses. I am unable to say more than a few words without pausing to have my ventilator fill my lungs with air. Additionally, my voice is weak and does not carry very well. I recently realized that I have been physically unable to laugh for a few years now. It has been a difficult transition, I loved to socialize and commune with others.

My career which I loved on so many levels is forever gone. It provided me an intellectual and creative outlet as well as the privilege of caring for the sick. The wonder and power of healing invigorated me and gave my career purpose. It gave me the energy to stay late and go back to the hospital in the middle of the night for the emergency procedure. I miss the camaraderie of friends and colleagues.

I miss the ability to actively share in hobbies, activities and playtime with my family. Most of my free time prior to my illness was spent playing ball with my boys, preparing the riding arena and horse jumps for my wife and daughter, ball games, practices, horse shows, boating and hiking. I miss trail riding in the mountains with Kirsten. I miss our adventure filled vacations. Although, I am grateful to Kirsten that we are still able to vacation, thanks to her herculean efforts.

I miss embracing my loved ones when they are happy and when they are sad. I miss tucking my family in at night. We had quite a routine with playtime, reading, stories, tickles and prayers. After our children were fast asleep, I would sneak off to the barn and join Kirsten with a glass of wine. We would tuck the horses and ponies in for the night and then collapse on the couch. Kirsten would soon fall asleep, hastened by a foot massage. Evenings were my favorite part of the day.

With my facial muscles weakening and as I lose my ability to purse my lips around my ventilator mouthpiece, I am now weighing the pros and cons of getting a tracheostomy tube. A surgical procedure in which an incision is made in the front of my neck and a plastic tube permanently inserted into my airways. I am discerning the undue burden for my family of going on tracheostomy ventilation against hospice care with a resultant swift demise. I know full well their pain in losing me as I experienced the loss of my mom. The Holy Spirit will tell me when their burden overcomes their benefit from my physical existence. I am grateful for their help.

A new phenomenon I have experienced since my diagnosis is anxiety triggered when anything touches the front of my neck, a shirt collar that is pulled tight, a napkin or the chain from which my crucifix hangs. This hypersensitivity occurs in the precise location a tracheostomy would be placed, a cruel irony. At the same time, I am jubilant at the prospect of Heaven. Yet, I feel my work is not done. I feel I am being called to pull my loved ones in. I want them to know this jubilation and peace. My loved ones are limited to everyone.

My airways have been filling with secretion. There have been several episodes this past month. Most episodes were triggered by an aspiration while others were spontaneous. These episodes have lasted from hours up to a full twenty-four hours. This despite two machines I have to help me clear my airways as I cannot cough on my own. My social worker recently told me that they had never had a patient at the clinic with my respiratory function still on noninvasive ventilation. She encouraged me to schedule a tracheostomy, if that is my inclination, before it is too late.

This decision gives me pause, I will speak no more. A tracheostomy will put an end to my spoken words. My loved ones will no longer hear my voice, Words of love and encouragement. This decision would be easier if ALS had already taken my ability to speak. Speaking to my family and friends give me great joy. This ability to freely communicate makes me feel like I am not sick at all. At the same time, demands on them will be further taxed. Meanwhile, these episodes are scary for my family and I know I'm taking a chance. I wish that I could ease their anxiety. I am at peace. The prospect of these episodes and the episodes themselves raise no anxiety only peace. I will try to make it through Christmas. So it will be, January

2014 it is. Everything is as it should be. Once again, I am reminded of the words of St. Teresa:

> Let nothing trouble you,
> let nothing frighten you.
> All things are passing;
> God never changes.
> Patience obtains all things.
> He who possesses God lacks nothing:
> Only God suffices.

I am grateful that with all of this suffering, I am filled with gratitude; grateful that lost physical abilities were not wasted engaged in a virtual world of television, videogames and the internet. Friends would give me grief over all of my free time. I would joke that I did twelve-months of work in eight months. Similarly, I feel that I have lived a full life, eighty years in forty-seven. Somehow, I am happy and I am at peace, a gift from Lourdes.

I am filled with gratitude even as I am wasting away, intimately in touch with my mortality. I have been stripped of my abilities, my independence and any authority I once had, yet I am grateful. As I reflect each day on all that I am grateful for, I am grateful that I am otherwise healthy. I am grateful that I do not suffer from a hundred other comorbidities that would negatively impact my quality-of-life. I am grateful for my family's health.

I am grateful for all the wonderful memories from the adventurous vacations to ballgames, horse shows, and recitals. I am even grateful for all the stressful times in my life and all of the suffering. I now see that they kept me from going too far off course and eventually would change the trajectory of my spiritual life.

I am grateful for Dr. Brooks and his ALS clinic at the Carolinas Medical Center. I am grateful for the culture of hope and the respect for life that he has established there.

I am grateful for our community here in Gastonia, North Carolina. Although transplanted from the North, we are home here.

I am grateful that my sons have similar interests and enjoy playing sports together, each of them filling in for me. Thankful, that they still want me to coach and referee them. However limited I am now, I am most grateful that I am still able to fill my role as father.

I am grateful that they have a sister to look out for them and vice versa. I am grateful that my wife and daughter share a passion for horses and this common bond will keep them connected especially during the trying teen years. I pray that my wife and children will all be close friends for life. I am grateful for financial decisions that have allowed us to carry on with our lives, minimizing ALS's impact. Kirsten has been able to bolster the load that I once carried, all the while maintaining hers. I am most grateful for that.

I believe the restlessness that I felt prior to my illness was God wanting me to give more, and Him wanting to give me more. He wanted me to give something that the divorce of my parents, my mom's cancer and subsequent death, and the fulfillment of my childhood dreams and prayers did not; something that no amount of money could offer. In fact, money only makes this gift more difficult. He wanted me to give myself to Him. Once I did, I understood divorce, cancer, death, and suffering. I am grateful that ALS has given me another chance to do that. Through my suffering and through my deteriorating physical capabilities, I have gained so much more. I have gained a true happiness that can only be found in an intimate relationship with Christ. My cross is no cross at all, simply a life; a life I would not change with anyone's.

I realize now that, like my professional abilities, my physical gifts, my hobbies, and my wealth, my suffering, too, has been a gift. I recall the words of Pope Emeritus Benedict XVI: "Everything is a gift from God: it is only by recognizing this crucial dependence on the Creator that we will find freedom and peace."

Chapter Sixteen

Harnessing and Harnessed

To be grateful is to recognize the Love of God in everything He has given us - and He has given us everything. Every breath we draw is a gift of His love, every moment of existence is a grace, for it brings with it immense graces from Him.
—Thomas Merton

When I was healthy, I had a confidence that comes with success. I worked hard to obtain and continually develop my abilities and I worked hard in fulfilling my duties as a partner in a busy radiology practice. However, I knew my abilities and what I was doing at work was a gift and that it was all temporary. I was grateful to countless mentors, colleagues, and God. The ability to directly impact patients' lives through image guided procedures and interpretation of radiologic studies was always interesting and often exhilarating. The job was a privilege and I knew it.

I always had high expectations on myself as physician, husband, father, and friend. I found myself constantly trying to improve all aspects of myself and my environment, endlessly in search of improvement, innovation, and efficiencies. Placing these expectations on others has, at times, led to disappointment, frustration, and hurt. As I have lost my independence and my ability to improve, heal and innovate, these feelings are sometimes magnified. Strengthening my interior life has helped me lower my expectations of others. I am learning to focus on my sins and the needs of others, not the other way around.

I remember feeling sorrow for sick patients especially young patients with terminal disease, new diagnoses of cancer or severe trauma. I can remember an attractive woman in her mid-thirties, my age at the time, sitting in the hallway after having an MRI. I reviewed the MRI before she left. Seeing a large aggressive glioma and realizing that she only had a few months to live, the sadness left an impression on me.

When my health began to fail, I did not have self-pity and I did not feel like I was being punished. I did not focus on my suffering and lost abilities, things that were out of my control. I remained hopeful. After my ALS diagnosis, I was scared, for myself and my family. But I felt loved, by family, friends and also by God. They were my rock. They kept me going and kept me strong when my world was falling apart. In the calm that came with my diagnosis, my hope pivoted from a treatable disease to an eternity in Heaven.

Fortunately, much of my day is filled with joy. This joy comes from focusing my current abilities and my many blessings. Cherishing memories and lost abilities without regret, I find enhances the joy from my remaining abilities. Wonderful memories and higher-level thinking in addition to sight, hearing, taste, smell and the touch of a loved one remains and are all the better. But also, the joy comes from attaining the higher purpose. I have found meaning, and it all makes sense.

In many ways, I am happier today. Not many people would believe that a person having lost so much could be happy at all. This fact has been incredibly awakening to me personally. I was not one who sat down and read or watched television. I kept up with several medical journals, but rarely read for pleasure. I valued productivity, the tangible. I was an active participant in life. I prided myself in getting things done. If I sat down, I was reading radiologic studies at work, driving my car, mower or RTV working on our small horse farm. Mucking stalls, stacking hay, cutting down trees, splitting and stacking wood, this was my time for taking it all in.

I have found that lasting happiness and peace do not come from material things or job, hobby, vacation or even another individual. They can all be good things and may bring temporary happiness. Experience tells me that enduring happiness, inner joy and peace come with abundant love and mercy. These pillars of a self-actualized life spring forth from a field of abundant gratitude and a Christ-centered life. When I am focused on all that I am grateful for and when I am focused on Him, I am bursting, invincible.

ALS has changed me or rather has opened me up to change. In spite of the daily physical suffering and frustrations, the lost abilities, and my lack of independence, I have an inner joy and empowerment like I never had when I was able bodied. Once touched by the Holy Spirit, there is no looking back. This is not to say that I do not lose my focus and sin, but seeing God in all things, makes denial much more difficult.

The challenge is in sharing this new-found perspective. Many I love most do not want to walk with me down this path. They want to compartmentalize my illness as an anomaly. They do not want to think too much about it or try to make sense of it. It is too painful to make that journey especially when we are able bodied and still powerful. Sadly, our faith is placed, all too often, in this life. It is a challenge to get to the point where we see illness and suffering as an opportunity: An opportunity to grow, to give, to get it right while there is still time. I feel that my blessings are stronger than ever.

I hear shallow goings on about this activity and that, all self gratifying without any substance, service or gratitude. Without appreciating the beauty of the universe, all life, the human mind and soul, we cannot see the big picture of life. Sadly, below the surface of activities and acquisitions is emptiness and restlessness. We let inconveniences, injustices, disappointments, and failure affect our outlook and we miss out on so much. I should know, I was a disciple of this way of life.

At the same time, my family and I have been the recipients of tremendous kindness and compassion by family, friends and our community. Their assistance and camaraderie have been invaluable. God is working through them. I am particularly touched by their generosity at our Marty Party, a night of music and celebration, where we raised $75,000 for ALS resarch. I hope to pay back their generosity. They have my prayers.

I am compelled to help others grow and go deeper. I am patient and persistent despite being at times rebuffed. In their defense, the mindset of some tells them their mortality is in the distant future and can be addressed later. Also, conventional wisdom is that death is dark and terrifying. My grandmother is afraid to die. She does not want to be "put in a coffin and placed in a hole in the ground." My disabilities, imminent mortality and lucid mind make it much easier for me to devote my time and energy developing my faith and attempting to make sense of it is all.

Society tells them that I am an outlier. We take comfort in the masses who agree with us, admittedly so do I. But, when we meet our maker, we will be alone with Him. Those we relied on to justify our misplaced values and emboldened our false sense of power will not be there. There will be no one to blame and no one to corroborate our denial, yet we deny and justify. We are weak, but with Christ, we are strong.

When we are able to physically alter our environment or have the financial means to obtain any and all material goods that catch our fancy, we feel entitled and empowered. Power is a potent and strongly addictive drug. We instinctively try to hold onto that power any way we can, at any cost. We disregard or all together lose our dignity and our moral compass. So we discredit any threat to that sense of power. ALS has robbed me of my false sense of power, opening me up to the Holy Spirit. I am grateful and once again unfairly blessed.

CHAPTER SEVENTEEN

TRUE LIBERTY

Take, Lord, and receive all my liberty, my memory, my understanding and my entire will--all I have and call my own. You have given all to me. To you, Lord, I return it. Everything is yours; do with it what you will. Give me only your love and your grace. That is enough for me.

—St. Ignatius of Loyola

Relativism justified my sins when my lifestyle was not congruent with Church teachings. Let's face it, religion with its doctrines and imperatives is inconvenient and the implication of our sinful ways on our eternity is frightening. How do we wrap our minds around these truths let alone embrace them in our increasingly secular, materialistic and hedonistic society? Better to stick our heads in the sand and plead ignorance, right? Unfortunately, ignorance does not excuse us from the law of the land, natural law and the imperatives articulated by Jesus Christ.

Relativism is dangerous. This doctrine teaches that knowledge, truth and morality are not absolute and rather exist in relation to culture, society and historical context. We only have to be good relative to someone else or societal norms. We can always think of someone else with worse behavior. Because everyone else is doing it does not make it right. This thought process leads to an even greater sin, thinking of ourselves as godlike.

I was heavily burdened with attachments, pride and haste. ALS, in severing my attachments, got me to refocus my life. I was finally able to dedicate the time and effort in developing my soul, bringing me graces and gifts of the Holy Spirit. Pride, laziness and material distractions kept me from putting in the necessary time and effort. Pride had me buying into relativism, justifying my spiritual laziness and denial of truth. With the perspective and humility of a child, the Mass, prayer, and meditation are my rock.

We are constantly bombarded with material goods, messages telling us we should have more. We deserve more. These images lead to sinful thoughts and desires creating a fertile ground for more serious sin. This is an impossible landscape to find lasting happiness and peace. Even the poorest of us living in this country have basic needs and a quality of life superior to most of the population on our planet, yet we are unhappy. We compare ourselves to those that have more. We do not consider the unfairness of the overwhelming majority of human beings on earth that have much less and we certainly don't compare our own unfair quality-of-life with the hardships of generations past.

I have had the unfair privilege of sharing time with Bishop Curlin, the personal confessor of Mother Teresa. Bishop Curlin had a close relationship with her both when she visited the United States and in Calcutta, India. Upon her death, he flew in Air Force One with then-First Lady Hillary Clinton for her funeral in Calcutta. I speculate that Mother Theresa gravitated to Bishop Curlin because of his incredible humility and devotion to those who are vulnerable. The Bishop lives simply, filling his days caring for the poor and the sick even to this day with a heart condition and cancer.

Bishop Curlin has shared many remarkable stories about Mother Teresa on different occasions. He also shares some wonderful and humorous stories, experiences with Pope John Paul II. At lunch this week, May 2013, Bishop Curlin shared a story that truly hit home. When the Bishop was a young priest, an older priest shared a story with him. This older priest, along with hundreds of Catholic Priests were rounded up and placed in the Dachau Concentration Camp in Nazi Germany.

One day, several priests were lined up and timed while they ran a certain distance. If they did not beat an arbitrary time, they would be gassed and then incinerated. A Nazi officer walking along the line of priests, randomly shot and killed a priest while they were waiting in line. When the Nazi soldier reached the priest telling the story, he pointed the gun to his face. A higher ranking Nazi officer pushed the soldiers arm down as he was pulling the trigger. The gun fired into the priest's leg.

This priest was spared the gas chamber and survived the concentration camp.

Twenty-two years after the war while walking in Munich, the priest saw the soldier who shot him approaching. The Nazi soldier recognized the priest and froze. The priest saw the fear in his eyes as he could have turned him in for his war crimes. Instead, he put his arms around him and whispered to him that he forgave him. The former Nazi soldier tormented with grief over what he had done during the war, experienced immediate relief from his burden with those words from the priest.

Love and forgive everyone and let Christ sort out the details. We can let go of that burden. Too often we seek justice for others. Yet we expect mercy from others and above all from God. We feel justified in our acts of non-love to the point that they become subconscious.

This mandate to love and forgive is not a tall order when we are well rested, well fed, all of our needs are met and everything is going our way. It is certainly no saintly act to be kind under these circumstances. However, when we are in pain, tired, hungry, fearful, when our feelings are hurt or things are not going our way and we face evil, then it is much more of a challenge to stay positive and take the high road.

When we are asked to endure unnecessary suffering, then it is even more of a challenge. It is easy to see Christ in others when life is going well and everyone is playing nice. In dark times, however, when others disappoint or mistreat us, a loved one or complete strangers as in the Boston Marathon bombing or the Holocaust, then it becomes more of a challenge to see Christ in that individual or group.

It is these very moments that we dread so much that we should anticipate and welcome. These moments are our opportunity to achieve greatness for ourselves and others, by exemplifying Christ's love. I am reminded of the merciful priest concentration camp victim and mentor of Bishop Curlin. We are called to manifest mercy even at these weak moments. When we do this, the rewards are immediate and everlasting.

I have learned through ALS to try to embrace suffering. It has taught me to move outside of myself, to be compassionate, and to forgive. My ALS and my suffering are a gift. True liberty is not relativism or materialism. True liberty is mercy and gratitude.

CHAPTER EIGHTEEN

WONDER AND SUFFERING

We shall never learn to know ourselves except by endeavoring to know God; for, beholding His greatness, we realize our own littleness; His purity shows us our foulness; and by meditating upon His humility we find how very far we are from being humble.

— St. Teresa of Avila

To wonder is to speculate curiously, to be filled with admiration, amazement or awe. When I was a child, I was filled with wonder, curious about everything. Known as the inquisitor, I drove my family crazy with questions. This innate inquiry guided me to a career in medicine. I was fascinated with the human body and intrigued by the prospect of caring for the sick, still unaware of the intoxicating power of healing that was in store.

As an adult, I am again filled with wonder. Wonder at the miracle of my children, my wife, this beautiful living planet Earth, the universe, the Mass, our Creator and suffering. Think about human beings, our minds, our capabilities, our accomplishments, our potential and our souls; our capacities to love, create, build and explore, to inquire; our almost innate sense of God, a Creator from the very beginning of man. Now look up and gaze at the billions and billions of stars. Telescopes allow us to observe galaxies and birthing stars as well as stars burning out. The dominant theory in science suggests the universe is expanding. Marvel and wonder at it all. All the complexities and contingencies in the universe and in life, it is overwhelming, too much for most to contemplate. This certainly does not seem random to me. A compelling argument for God, wouldn't you agree?

All matter in the universe is made up of atoms. Atoms are made up of energy. Energy possessing different properties depending on its' arrangements and associations. All that we see is energy. From this perspective, it is not hard to imagine bread and wine, energy, becoming the body and blood of Christ, energy, through transubstantiation. This miracle occurs daily throughout the world. Christ is made flesh again just as he was 2000 years ago. Distracted with the material world, how many of us fail to give witness as we fail to marvel at the beauty of this sacrament.

I feel like I can recall all of the times I have been to Mass and received Holy Communion, as crazy as that sounds. The Mass is much more than readings from the Bible and a homily or sermon. Something must be happening there that leaves a permanent imprint on our mind. We are giving ourselves, offering ourselves to God as is Christ. Christ is offering up his body at each Mass performed each day around the world, in atonement for our sins, just as He did on Calvary two thousand years ago. We are offering up our lives, to live selflessly as He taught us and unworthy, we have the incredible opportunity to take His flesh and blood into our bodies. There is nothing in this life that is more powerful.

The prevalence of suffering is astonishing, a wonder really. If we are so inclined, technologies allow us opportunities to tune into suffering experienced in our families, our communities and throughout our planet. Thank God, Christ gave meaning and purpose to suffering. Suffering is an essential part of who we are as human beings. The absence of suffering would strip free will of any meaning. Any decision we made would have the same result, the absence of suffering. With great difficulty, it is for this reason that I am choosing to make unpopular decisions in setting limits and disciplining my children even as I am dying.

A disciplined diet is suffering for many. Restraint of any kind often involves suffering yet usually is good. Disciplined exercise, work habits, parenting and children all involve suffering to some extent; nevertheless they all bear much fruit. A surgeon must cut through healthy tissue, injuring it, in order to cut out diseased tissue. Chemotherapeutic agents and radiotherapy destroy healthy tissue along with the diseased neo plastic tissue. If an evil means does not justify a good end, then we must conclude that suffering quite often is paradoxically good.

Without suffering, our sense of conscience would quickly erode. Discernment of good from evil would become nearly impossible. Society as we know it could not exist without suffering. One must conclude then that our suffering is or at least can be a good thing. Suffering is the engine of higher thinking, ingenuity, philosophy and faith. God became man, was raised in poverty, chose to live with the sick and the poor, and suffered a prolonged and especially gruesome death, opening the gates to Heaven. It can be a wonderful thing, this suffering.

Once we understand that suffering can bring happiness, even joy and inner peace, we can achieve great things for ourselves and others. Suffering brings a rewarding career, a successful marriage, well-adjusted God fearing children, and, most importantly, eternity. As Matthew relates in the Gospel:

Jesus said to his disciples, "If any want to become my followers, let them deny themselves and take up their cross and follow me. For those who want to save their life will lose it, and those who lose their life for my sake will find it. For what will it profit them if they gain the whole world but forfeit their life? Or what will they give in return for their life? For the Son of Man is to come with his angels in the glory of his Father, and then he will repay everyone for what has been done. Truly I tell you, there are some standing here who will not taste death before they see the Son of Man coming in his kingdom."

Despite the gospel teaching, the purpose of suffering, however, is not always readily apparent to us. As a child, I hated taking a nap. I did not want to miss out. I would cry and scream, suffering from my perspective. Yet I would awaken with renewed energy and spirit. Disease, death, senseless atrocities and natural disasters do not make sense to our little minds. Where is the meaning? Just as something as wonderful as a nap is suffering to a child, one day it will all make sense and we will be glad. Maybe the purpose of these sufferings is simply God giving us an opportunity to bring out the best in humanity.

In my experience, the path of least resistance is usually the wrong path. Success was never sweeter and life never more joyful than following a period of suffering. If only we approached suffering as it really is, an opportunity for improvement, ingenuity, and eternity. Suffering brings us back to the beginning. Suffering brings us back to Christ.

MODERN DILEMMA

With all of our discoveries, advancements and technologies, is suffering any less today? I think not. The average lifespan has doubled in the United States in the past 150 years and we now enjoy a wealth and quality-of-life the world has never known. Yet, suffering remains and the happiness of our citizens has been stagnant. In fact, many impoverished nations around the world report happiness levels that surpass our own. With our increased lifespan, one could argue that our accumulative suffering is even greater today.

Unfortunately, many of us choose to insulate ourselves in an attempt to lessen the pain of suffering. No one would argue that technologies have the potential to, and often do, improve the quality of our lives. But these technologies also have the potential to harm us. Temptation was never so incessant and vices were never so accessible. We distract ourselves with a virtual world of video games, movies, television, sports, fantasy sports, social media, music, and so on. We are inundated, tempted, and distracted at every turn. The allure of these technologies can be powerful, and we must make a conscious effort to limit them.

We are attracted to a virtual world as it shields us from being an active participant in our families and communities. The irony is that our personal suffering would be more manageable if we would only reassess our priorities; putting people before material things, realities and responsibilities ahead of a virtual reality.

Our constant desire to avoid suffering is fruitless, and usually just creates more suffering. The only existence without suffering is in Heaven. We need not seek out suffering, but we are called to embrace it, as Christ did. Fortunately, suffering brings opportunity to deepen our understanding of life, giving it meaning and purpose. Self-pity is opportunity lost. Christ calls us to be saints, to be like Him. Therefore, we must bear our cross and suffer, as He suffered. There is great opportunity in this suffering.

A natural instinct when we experience a setback, disappointment, or devastating tragedy is to become filled with self-pity. Often we ask why we got such a raw deal while others have it so good. Maybe this is because we are not in tune with the suffering and struggle of others. When we tune into the suffering of others and pray for them, our suffering does not seem that bad. More than simple awareness, empathizing with the suffering of others allows our suffering to dissipate. Going further, praying for those who suffer, empowers us to not only conquer our suffering but has eternal consequences.

EPITOME

In life, we need to continually develop three things, in balance: the body, the mind, and the soul. I spent most of my life developing my mind and body. A strong and active spiritual life brings serenity and the graces to utilize our gifts to fulfill Divine Providence. Proper stewardship of our own bodies and minds and our stewardship of all creation will naturally be aligned with God's will.

It took ALS to get me to develop my soul.

As a child, I hated missing out. I kicked and screamed at nap time. I recall protests from my crib like they were yesterday. Likewise, as a young adult, basking in the social outlet, I rarely wanted to leave a party early. As a husband and a father of a young family, faced with an ALS diagnosis, that familiar feeling of missing out arose in me once again. I was sad that I would miss out on watching my children grow up, milestones in their lives, growing old with my wife. I was leaving behind a young wife and the idea of her remarrying did not sit well, at first. Now, I hope that she does find someone to spend the rest of her life with. Once I strengthened my faith in the afterlife, I was no longer sad for myself.

These days I have much time for prayer, reflection, and contemplation. As I reflect on my life experiences, I see that my happiest times have been when I found balance in my life.

An interesting career that is rewarding materially and intellectually and offers plenty of time off for family, exercise and hobbies can provide tremendous happiness; the American dream, right? I can tell you, without actively cultivating a rich spiritual life, this veneer of happiness will not bring peace. Having lost control of my body, my ability to work, my independence, and my ability to breathe without a machine, I have found peace that I never knew when I was able bodied.

My only regret is that I cannot do more physically for my wife and children.

My suffering, which started as a steady drip, developed over three years into a hurricane. When I finally received my ALS diagnosis, I reached the eye of the hurricane coming to a peculiar calm and peace.

Now, in the aftermath of the storm as I assess the devastation, I have a keener sense of the beauty and miracle of life. Miracles abound, from the birthing of human babies to the birthing of stars.

After seemingly fallen so far, why am I not filled with anger and self-pity? Instead of focusing on lost abilities and stature, I am filled with joy and peace. Never was I content with the status quo. I was constantly in search of improvements and efficiency, reevaluating my approach and perspective. Constantly looking to move the ball forward, I spend much of my time in the clouds, with lofty goals, ideas, and prayers.

The eagerness and curiosity of a child leads me each day. I continue to educate myself and discover. Daily, I work to develop my soul. Each morning starts with a Gospel reading and reflection with prayers and meditation throughout the day. My caregivers and I do everything we can to maintain my body with nutrition, medication, sleep, passive exercise, range-of-motion drills, massage chair sessions, and a percussion vest that brings fluid up from my airways. All of this maintains my balance of mind, body, and soul.

My innate inquiry, which annoyed my siblings as a child, has served me well by strengthening my faith. I was being called to go deeper, more than simply attend Sunday Mass with my family. My illness, in giving me time and opening me to counsel and steadfast prayer has brought me this third piece, a strengthened interior life. This balance of actively exercising mind, body, and soul is the granite foundation on which to build a productive, fulfilling life. Balance and gratitude allows us to accept and carry our cross as He did, bringing peace.

Prior to my diagnosis, I had a keen awareness of God and the afterlife. Nevertheless, I was heavily committed to this life. Heaven was somewhere up in the sky. The imagery of the blue sky and white clouds or the setting sun with the orange red sky is still quite vivid. I am not sure when it happened, sometime over the past few years since my ALS diagnosis, perhaps it was during my pilgrimage to Lourdes France, I began to understand Heaven to be right here amongst us. Heaven was no longer up in the sky, tucked away in some corner of in the universe. Heaven appeared as the matrix of energy that is all around us, that is us . . . that is veiled to us. Heaven is an unveiling. In the beginning, I only gained a glimpse of this when celebrating the Mass. In time, I would know this reality in meditation and prayer. Connecting with this reality warms my soul with increased frequency. Fear of my mortality and the supernatural eternity that terrified me as a young man have turned to joy.

ALS severed my attachments to my career, my many hobbies,

adventure vacations, many acquaintances and colleagues. Faith and reason helped me recognize that my suffering could provide an opportunity to strengthen my interior life and help others.

The void created by my abruptly truncated physical abilities and career had thrown my triune of mind, body and soul out of balance. Fortunately, spiritual growth, continued intellectual growth, and the outstanding care I receive from my wife and children, friends, and caregivers have helped me maintain my balance. My severed attachments to this life have strengthened my attachments to the afterlife and Christ bringing me peace and joy like never before.

This discovery of the incredible opportunity in suffering did not happen overnight, and it did not happen without effort. Daily reflection and prayer are essential as we are conditioned by society to be short-sighted and distracted. When I first started praying the Rosary, it was laborious. In time, with practice and persistence, I was able to gain insight, nourished by the fruits of its mysteries: sorrow for sins, purity, courage, patience, perseverance, humility, love of neighbor, poverty, obedience, joy in finding Jesus, faith, hope, love of God, grace of a happy death, trust in Mary's intercession, openness to the Holy Spirit, to Jesus through Mary, repentance and trust in God, a desire for holiness, and Adoration.

Through the counsel of Jerry Schmitt, KM, I have learned much about the Mass. His insight has taught me, among other things, how to be *in* the Mass rather than simply at Mass. Previously, the Mass felt long especially while managing three young children chafing at the bit. Now, the Mass is not long enough, seemingly lasting only moments.

In many ways, I am happier today. Not many people would believe that a person having lost so much could be happy at all. This fact has been incredibly awakening to me. I was not one who sat down and read or watched television. I kept up with several medical journals, but rarely read for pleasure. I valued productivity, the tangible. I was always on the go. I prided myself on getting things done. If I sat down, I was reading radiologic studies at work, driving my car, mower, or RTV, working on our small horse farm. Mucking stalls, stacking hay, cutting down trees, splitting and stacking wood, this was my time for taking it all in.

As I reflect on my life, I do not miss the fancy hotels and restaurants, adventure vacations, work, hobbies, and all the other things I loved so much at the time. I miss the chores, physically helping Kirsten and our children, the house, farm and all of our pets. I only yearn for platonic intimacy with family, friends, those in need and Christ. I am grateful for all of my life, even ALS . . . especially ALS.

The gentle tug on my soul waxed with my illness. My diagnosis came on the eighteenth anniversary of my mother's death. I could feel her calling me home. In my grief and despair, turning to the Church was as natural as returning to the comfort of my mom's arms. ALS was my eternal life-saver, I was being pulled in from turbulent waters. My Lourdes miracle gave me the graces to embrace my cross. Once I let go of lost abilities and did not look back, I derived renewed peace and a deeper joy from my remaining abilities. What I valued before, productivity and activity is now lost. Yet even now, I am happy and grateful, in many ways more so than before.

Quieting myself in order to appreciate the boundless beauty of life and all creation, brings joy. Turning off the noise and the emotions, and listening to God's word, lights my path. When my thoughts are aligned with His, my thoughts, words and actions flow with ease. Life becomes simple and incredibly beautiful.

This awareness tugged at me to do something more, something significant while I still had time. My illness and life experiences have taught me that suffering can be managed, conquered, and become a powerful tool. Society tells us that suffering is an evil and should be avoided at all cost. I have learned that suffering is often a good thing if we only look at it through a different lens, God's lens. Just as a child fails to see the good in chores and homework, as adults we often fail to see the good in suffering, in bearing our cross. If we truly believe in Heaven and that our lives are but a moment in time, our mortality and suffering becomes bearable.

After ten years of postgraduate training and eleven years of practice, I was highly trained and my skills were honed. I had so much more to give. Being a positive contributor to society is no more a guarantee of longevity as is a negative contributor to society a guarantee of an early demise. I have relearned that all that we do is in preparation for the next life. When this is our mantra, we gain clarity and life isn't so complicated. Fortunately, ALS brought me this clarity. Additionally, this serenity is rooted in hope. Hope for my wife and children, my entire family and friends, hope for the Church, this nation, and all of humanity.

Admittedly I was confused at first. My physical abilities were perishing and my physical world was closing with unrelenting speed. It seemed that it was all slipping away. Yet only now, after all this, have I attained this deep sense of joy and peace that no material "good" or achievement had ever brought me.

As nearly all of my physical abilities with the exception of the limited ability to speak and eat are now in the rearview mirror, my sense of self has not diminished. In fact, my sense of self has paradoxically risen. I have come to realize that the essence of who I am has not waned with my lost ability to ski, play tennis, golf, run, hike, walk, work, hug, take care of myself and those that I love or even breathe on my own. To my delight, the essence of me is not tied to an activity or a physical ability. The essence of me is my ability to trust, love, inquire, and learn. The essence of me is the essence of a child. The essence of a child is the essence of a human life. The essence of a life is to be a lifeline, an eternal lifeline, to one another.

***　　　　　***　　　　　***

Life has been unfair to me: unfairly good. My experiences have helped me realize that suffering was ubiquitous and that our time here was finite. With the exception of Heaven, suffering knows no boundaries. Every one of us suffers to some extent on a daily basis and will inevitably experience life-changing tragedies. Suffering yields not to any amount of money, fame, culture, religion, or even Jesus Christ Himself, although His was by choice. Christ invites us to carry our cross if we want to follow him. Fortunately our cross does not approximate the Passion. Our experience tells us that our physical bodies will end and science tells us our physical world, planet Earth will end. The good news is that all suffering will eventually end, unless of course, we are to spend eternity apart from God.

Originally, I thought my target audience would be my family. Then I thought patients, family and friends of patients might benefit. However, we all encounter struggles throughout each day with inevitable crises and tragedies. Therefore, this message of recognizing opportunity in suffering, in our personal cross, is for everyone.

I have lived a dream life. Yesterday I was an insecure child from a divided home. Today I have a beautiful, loving family. Yesterday there was confusion and doubt, now an immensely rewarding career and confidence. Well, that's not quite right. My career has been lost to ALS. I have lost the ability to hug my wife and children, wrestle, tickle, and play ball with my boys and ride horses with my wife and daughter. Gone are golf and tennis with friends, boating and snow skiing with family. Gone are my restlessness and my constant desire for *more*. Now there is only God and peace . . . at last.

Dying can be beautiful. Withering physically, professionally, and socially can be beautiful if it strengthens bonds of love and compassion. If the process of dying awakens a spirituality within us, a greater sense of the eternal, then dying can be a beautiful process.

I have lived a full life. I have achieved professional and financial success. I have built the family I had dreamed of. And yet, here, in my last days, perhaps ALS has been my greatest gift. This disease, this suffering, has allowed me to find the joy and peace of Christ. I am happy in His loving embrace.

About the Author

Martin J. D'Amore, MD, was born in Illinois in 1966. He earned his Bachelor degree from the University of Illinois. Marty received his medical degree is from Rush University Medical School in Chicago, performed his radiology residency at Loyola and his interventional radiology fellowship at Wake Forest Baptist Medical Center. Marty spent his entire eleven-year professionl career as an interventional radiologist in Gastonia, NC, just west of Charlotte, where he is an active member of St. Michael's parish. Marty, his wife, Kirsten, and their three children reside on a small horse farm in Gastonia.

***

One-hundred percent of the proceeds from this book will be donated to Belmont Abbey College, St. Michael's Catholic Church, the Marty Fund, and/or the Joe Martin ALS Foundation. If you are further interested in supporting ALS research and care for those afflicted with ALS, please consider making a donation to the Marty Fund (named after the author) or the Joe Martin ALS Foundation.

To donate to the Marty Fund, go to:

givecarolinas.org

Click the Donate Now button, then click on Neurological Disorders and select Marty's Fund from the drop down box.

To learn more or to make a donation to the the Joe Martin ALS Foundation, please visit:

joemartinalsfoundation.org

***

CPSIA information can be obtained
at www.ICGtesting.com
Printed in the USA
LVHW022320170820
663418LV00016B/1766